W9-CDT-744

Economics

Economics

Progression, Stagnation or Degeneration?

J.C. GLASS and W. JOHNSON

Iowa State University Press/Ames

J. C. Glass is Lecturer in Economics, University of Ulster at Coleraine.
W. Johnson is Lecturer in Economics, University of Ulster at Coleraine.

Published in the United States and Canada
by the Iowa State University Press, Ames, Iowa 50010

Published simultaneously in Great Britain by
Harvester Wheatsheaf, Hemel Hempstead, Hertfordshire HP2 4RG

Printed in England

First edition, 1989

Library of Congress Cataloging-in-Publication Data
Glass. J. Colin.
Economics — progression, stagnation, or degeneration? J. C. Glass and W. Johnson. — 1st ed.
ISBN 0 – 8138 – 0622 – 4
1. Economics — Methodology. I. Johnson. W. II. Title.
HB131.G57 1989
330.1 — dc19 89–2036

Contents

Preface

This book arose out of a common interest in the methodology of economics. Having enjoyed many discussions on methodological issues, we decided to include some coverage of these issues in certain undergraduate economics courses that we were teaching. Not only did our students respond favourably to this brief introduction to methodological issues, but some even suggested that we should write a book that would enable students to pursue their interest in this area. Consequently, we decided to write this book which, as the subtitle points out, is intended to provide an introduction to the methodological issues involved in assessing the growth of economic knowledge.

In writing the book, we very much appreciated the encouragement and comments received from our colleagues in the University of Ulster. In particular, we are grateful for the help given by James Brown of the Department of Philosophy. Sheila Dow, of Stirling University, kindly read the entire manuscript and provided us with constructive criticisms and valuable suggestions. To her we extend a special note of thanks and appreciation. We would also like to thank Professor Noretta Koertge for kindly providing us with English translations of her work published in German.

Sections of the book are forthcoming in 'Metaphysics, MSRP and Economics' *British Journal for the Philosophy of Science,* 39 (3), pp. 313-30, 1988. We are grateful to the Publishers and editor for permission to reproduce this material.

Finally, we wish to thank Adrienne McLaughlin and Carol Kealey for their cheerful, efficient typing of the Manuscript.

1 Introduction

Many students are drawn to the study of economics by the wide range of interesting topics (such as inflation, wages, unemployment, income distribution, resource allocation, economic growth, pollution, international trade, balance of payments, exchange rates, etc.) that are studied under the general heading of economics. In particular, many students are keen to take at least an introductory course in economics in order to enhance their understanding not only of how the economy works, but also of the problems involved in current public debates over government economic policy.

1.1 THE PROBLEM OF COMPETING THEORIES

Such students often expect to find decisive answers to the important economic questions which quickly emerge from the analysis of the above topics. They do not, however, have to progress very far into an introductory economics course before they discover that such decisive answers are lacking. Instead of finding that just one theory has been proposed to explain certain economic phenomena, they quickly discover that two or more rival theories have been advanced in an attempt to explain them, and that not only is there often considerable disagreement among the proponents of these theories, but also that these rival theories form the basis for very different (and even directly conflicting) economic policy recommendations.

Given that economics generates such competing theories, this immediately raises a very important question: how are these theories to be compared and evaluated so as to ascertain which theory is superior to the others? In other words, is there a methodological procedure which enables economics researchers not only to appraise each of these theories individually but also to rank them? This question, in turn, raises a further question: if such a ranking of theories is possible, does this automatically mean that the policy recommendations based upon these theories are to be ranked accordingly?

1.2 THE INTEREST IN OBTAINING ANSWERS TO METHODOLOGICAL QUESTIONS

In our teaching experience, even on introductory economics courses, we have found that students are very keen to discover what attempts have been made to answer these very important questions. Not only are they keen to know how a particular economic theory is appraised and compared with other economic theories, they are especially keen to know whether or not economic knowledge is progressing, stagnating or degenerating. Thus, in our teaching experience (not only on introductory economics courses but also on more advanced economics courses and on refresher courses for non-university teachers of economics), we have found that there is considerable interest in obtaining an understanding of the important issues involved in appraising economic theories, comparing economic theories, and assessing the growth of economic knowledge.

Unfortunately, however, the discussion of these important issues is generally confined to advanced, specialist courses (or advanced books and journal articles) on the methodology of economics, where the *methodology of economics* refers not simply to the methods used by economics researchers, but rather to the study of the reasoning behind the procedures that guide such researchers in theory appraisal, theory comparison, and assessing the growth of economic knowledge. Consequently, many students have been unable to pursue their interest in these important issues.

1.3 A DISCUSSION OF METHODOLOGICAL ISSUES FOR BEGINNERS

Faced with this situation, we decided to write a book which would provide a discussion of these important methodological issues at a level which is suitable for students who have completed no more than an introductory first-year university course in economics. Consequently, in writing this book, our aim has been to provide an introduction to these methodological issues which, on the one hand, does not require any more than an elementary knowledge of economics, (and, in contrast to most books on the methodology of economics, no prior knowledge of the philosophy of science or of the history of economic thought) and, on the other hand, still represents an adequate, accurate discussion of these important methodological issues.

As indicated by the subtitle of the book, our goal is *not* to assess whether economics is currently progressing, stagnating or degenerating, but rather to introduce students to the important methodological issues involved in assessing the growth of economic knowledge. Given this goal, the book concentrates mainly on what is known as the 'growth of knowledge' approach, and in particular examines the implications of adopting either Karl Popper's *falsificationist methodology* or Imre Lakatos's *methodology of scientific research programmes* (denoted for short as MSRP) in economics.

While both falsificationism and MSRP are discussed, the main emphasis is on Lakatos's MSRP as (we shall argue) this provides greater insight into the methodological problems associated with assessing the growth of economic knowledge than falsificationism does. In particular, we shall argue that MSRP provides an extremely useful framework for examining the difficulties that arise in comparing 'orthodox' economic theories (meaning those economic theories which are predominantly taught in western universities, polytechnics and schools) with 'Marxist' economic theories. (For the argument that MSRP provides important insight into recent developments in econometrics, see Gilbert [1986].)

1.4 THE PEDAGOGIC APPROACH

The book has been deliberately structured so as to provide a gradual, cumulative build-up of knowledge on methodological issues. Thus we start from the position, described above, in which new students of economics quickly encounter the problem of competing economic theories. In these circumstances students want to know why such disagreements cannot be resolved empirically by an appeal to the relevant evidence. In other words, they want to know why economic explanations and policy recommendations are not based exclusively on theories which have not only been derived from empirical evidence, but have also been objectively established as true on the basis of this empirical evidence. This 'common-sense' view of economic knowledge is examined in Chapter 2 on *Inductivism*, and is shown to be beset with major problems when one tries to put it into practice.

The existence of these problems still leaves us with the question of what economic explanations and economic policy recommendations are to be based upon, and how the merits of competing theories are to be compared and evaluated. Faced with the problems of inductivism, a pragmatic response might be simply to concentrate on those theories which predict well in relation to the empirical evidence. This approach (which has enjoyed a certain popularity amongst economists—most notably in the writings of the economics Nobel laureate Milton Friedman) is examined in Chapter 3 on *Instrumentalism*, but it in turn is shown to have serious shortcomings.

An alternative, and in many ways a more satisfactory, approach to the problems associated with inductivism is *Falsificationism*, which is considered in Chapter 4. This methodology advocates that each theory be rigorously exposed to empirical tests and any theory which is falsified by these tests be rejected, so that only those theories which are not falsified are then retained. Falsificationism too, however, has its problems and, what is more, the history of economics has shown that theories are in fact retained even when they have been falsified.

The limitations of falsificationism and a rationale for the retention of falsified theories are explained in Chapter 5, *From Falsificationism to Lakatosian Research Programmes*. In Chapter 5 the reader is also introduced to Lakatos's Methodology of Scientific Research Programmes (MSRP), which endeavours to overcome the problems of falsificationism by emphasising, amongst other things, that theories should not only be considered individually but also as part of an overall research programme which incorporates a number of related theories.

Chapter 6, *Lakatos's Methodology of Scientific Research Pro-*

grammes, which provides a more detailed exposition of MSRP, is followed by two chapters which discuss the implications of adopting MSRP in economics. In Chapter 7, *Implications of Adopting MSRP in Economics—I*, the discussion relates to problems of appraisal within a given research programme, whereas in Chapter 8, *Implications of Adopting MSRP in Economics—II*, the discussion relates to problems of appraising rival research programmes such as the 'orthodox' and 'Marxist' economics research programmes mentioned above.

In order to enhance the understanding of each of the above methodological procedures, extensive use has been made of economic illustrations. Since it is intended that the book can be readily understood by students who have completed no more than a first-year university course in economics, it should be noted that these economic illustrations are such that only an elementary knowledge of economics is required to understand them. In this respect, the book provides, particularly in its discussion of MSRP, novel and extensive illustrations of what we have called the 'orthodox' and 'Marxist' research programmes. Moreover, since Marx's economics is often not taught in western universities, we have included an outline of some important features of Marx's economics in Section 8.3 which, together with the further discussion of Marx's economic analysis in Sections 8.4 and 8.5, will enable us to highlight the important differences between the 'orthodox' and 'Marxist' economics research programmes.

To round off our discussion of methodologies in the growth of knowledge tradition, we have included two chapters which examine, respectively, the methodological viewpoints of Thomas Kuhn and Paul Feyerabend. Thus, Chapter 9 examines *Kuhn's Normal Science and Revolutionary Science* and Chapter 10 examines *Feyerabend's Methodological Anarchism.*

With respect to Chapter 9, it should be noted that Kuhn's work not only historically preceded, but also influenced that of Lakatos (which is discussed in Chapters 5-8). However, while Kuhn's work predates that of Lakatos, we have deliberately placed our discussion of Lakatos immediately after the discussion of falsificationism, so as to reap the benefits of an uninterrupted emphasis on the falsificationist and Lakatosian methodological viewpoints, before discussing Kuhnian methodology. Essentially we feel that there are good pedagogic reasons for examining the falsificationist and

Lakatosian methodologies in sequence first, and then using this methodological discussion as a background for the examination of Kuhn's and Feyerabend's methodologies. Chapter 11, the final chapter of the book, provides as titled *Concluding Comments*.

Note that our discussion of the various methodologies has the goal of providing an examination of the implications of adopting any of these methodologies in economics. While the adoption of a particular methodology will not provide economics researchers with precise guidance as to how to solve research problems, the adoption of a particular methodology will inevitably suggest ways of both *approaching* and *appraising* their research activity. This is so even if the author of the particular methodology initially put the emphasis on *description* (and hence initially aimed at providing an accurate description of how research activity proceeded in the past) rather than on *prescription* (and hence initially aimed at providing researchers with advice on how to proceed so as to promote the growth of scientific knowledge). Clearly it is only to be expected that a descriptive knowledge of highly successful past research activity will have prescriptive implications for the way in which researchers should proceed currently in order to promote scientific advance.

It should also be noted that, in our discussion of the methodologies contained in this book, we have not been concerned with highlighting the respective *demarcation criteria* that the authors of these methodologies have proposed for separating science from non-science. While our discussion implicitly views economics as a science, we feel that the important methodological issue for economics is the development of objective appraisal criteria (which will enable economics researchers to appraise theories, compare theories and assess the growth of economic knowledge) rather than distinguishing between what is scientific and what is non-scientific.

However, while we implicitly accept that economics is a science, and hence consider it legitimate to examine the implications of adopting various methodologies in economics that were initially developed with reference to the physical sciences, our discussion makes it clear that there are obvious differences between a social science such as economics and a long-standing mature physical science such as physics. (For an interesting discussion of the implications of applying demarcation criteria to economics, see Sassower [1986].)

Finally, it should be noted that a summary has been provided at the end of each chapter. Also, in order to enhance the flow of the discussion, only major bibliographical references have been included in the text. Consequently, additional references for further reading are provided at the end of each chapter.

2 Inductivism

In Chapter 1 we noted that new students of economics want to know why the problem of choice amongst competing economic theories cannot be resolved empirically by an appeal to the relevant evidence. Often behind this query there tends to be a widely-held, 'common-sense' view that the theories over which the disagreements occur have in the first place been derived from factual evidence, and that it should therefore be possible to assess objectively which theory best conforms to the factual evidence. Since this 'common-sense' view of economic knowledge can be expressed more formally as the methodological standpoint known as *inductivism*, a response to the above query will inevitably involve an examination of inductivism. Consequently we shall now proceed to a detailed examination of inductivism.

A starting point

In order to aid our understanding of the methodological standpoint known as inductivism, we shall first construct a state of affairs to be explained and then examine how the inductivist proceeds to explain this state of affairs. Thus, let us assume that good x is bought and sold in a particular market (with this market being defined as the set of arrangements enabling buyers and sellers to negotiate the exchange of good x). Also, let us assume that we are faced with the question: why did the total quantity of good x demanded by all consumers of good x, in this market, decrease each consecutive week during the first quarter of 1986?

Now that we are faced with a question to be answered, or a state of affairs to be explained, how do we proceed? What method of procedure shall we adopt in order to investigate the behaviour of consumers purchasing good x? One answer is that our investigation of consumer purchasing behaviour should begin with the observation of facts and then, on the basis of the empirical evidence provided by the observed facts, arrive at a general conclusion about these facts. In other words, our investigation of consumer purchasing behaviour should rely heavily on the empirical evidence provided by observations of consumers purchasing good x, with the observed facts acting as a guide to lead us into a general conclusion that, in turn, will help us to explain why the demand for good x decreased each consecutive week during the first quarter of 1986. Since this is a frequently proposed method of procedure, known as the *inductivist procedure* (because it is based on *inductive reasoning* whereby the observed facts lead us, or induce us, into a general conclusion about these facts), let us examine it in somewhat more detail.

2.1 THE INDUCTIVIST PROCEDURE: FROM OBSERVATION TO THEORY

The inductivist procedure, as noted above, essentially consists of making observations of facts and then, on the basis of this empirical evidence, reaching a general conclusion about these facts. Clearly, at first sight, this method of procedure seems to be most reasonable and reliable. In particular, it appears to possess the desirable property of objectivity.

Nothing subjective appears to be involved in the inductivist procedure. We simply go to a supermarket, where good x may be purchased, and start making observations without any preconceived notions as to the relative importance of the observed facts. The observed facts are then faithfully recorded without any deliberate selection. This objective process of observation and recording is then repeated many times, both in this supermarket and other supermarkets (where good x may be purchased), until we have obtained a large number of observation statements.

The next step is to reach a general conclusion on the basis of the evidence provided by our observations. In doing so, note that nothing subjective appears to be involved here either. The inductive reasoning is essentially objective. It is the observed facts, rather than some subjective opinion, that lead us into a general conclusion. Also, note that the general conclusion is not made on the shaky, unreliable basis of a small number of observations. The general conclusion is only reached on the basis of a large number of observation statements which, in turn, have been obtained under a wide variety of conditions (by making observations at different times and in different supermarkets).

As an example, let us assume that, on the basis of our large number of observation statements, we have reached the general conclusion that the total quantity of good x demanded per week (denoted as Q_{dx}) by all consumers of good x is related to the price per unit of good x, which we shall denote as P_x. (For simplicity, we shall assume that P_x remains constant within any given week but can vary between weeks.) In particular, let us assume that the relation is such that Q_{dx} will increase (decrease) as P_x decreases (increases). Moreover, let us assume that none of our recorded observation statements conflict with this general conclusion. In other words, let us assume that, in all situations observed, the total quantity of good x demanded by consumers of good x was always related to the price of good x in the manner described by our general conclusion. Thus, on the basis of the empirical evidence, we have arrived at the general conclusion that Q_{dx} is inversely related to P_x.

Singular statements and universal statements

Now that we have a specific example of the inductivist procedure, we can introduce some additional terminology that will help to clarify our discussion. To do this note, in the above example, that the process of inductive reasoning commenced with observation statements and ended with a general conclusion (with the observation statements being used to lead us, or induce us, into this general conclusion). In particular, note that the observation statements are statements that refer to the behaviour of consumers purchasing good x at a *particular* place (some specific supermarket) at a *particular* time (the time and the date when the observations were made), whereas the *general* conclusion is a statement asserting something about the behaviour of consumers purchasing good x at *all* places and at *all* times (with the assertion being that the total quantity of good x demanded per week by all consumers of good x, at *all* places and at *all* times, is inversely related to the price per unit of good x).

Since statements that refer to a particular situation at a particular place at a particular time are known as *singular statements*, then our observation statements can be classified as singular statements. Also, since statements that refer to all events of a particular kind in all places and at all times are known as *universal statements*, then our general conclusion can be classified as a universal statement. Consequently, with reference to the above example, we can now state that the process of inductive reasoning commenced with singular statements and ended with a universal statement.

Explanation in the inductivist procedure

Returning to our discussion of the inductivist procedure, recall that we set out to explain why the total quantity of good x demanded by all consumers of good x, in the given market, decreased each consecutive week during the first three months of 1986. Also recall that, as a first step in attempting to provide the desired explanation, we used the inductivist procedure to generalize from a large number of singular statements to the universal statement that Q_{dx} is inversely related to P_{x}. If, as a second step, we now regard this universal statement as a universal *theory* or *hypothesis* of demand for good x, we can then proceed to demonstrate how this (simple) theory or hypothesis of demand can be used to provide an explanation of why the demand for good x decreased each consecutive week during the first quarter of 1986.

As we shall see, the explanation consists of a logical deduction whose premises consist of our simple theory of demand plus (singular) statements describing the situation under investigation (with the latter statements being known as *initial conditions*), and whose conclusion is a statement of what was to be explained (the consecutive weekly decreases in the demand for good x during the first quarter of 1986). For example, given the premises:

(1) The total quantity of good x demanded per week by all consumers of good x is inversely related to the price per unit of good x.

(2) The market for good x is defined as the set of arrangements enabling buyers and sellers to negotiate the exchange of good x.

(3) The price per unit of good x, paid by each consumer of good x in the market defined in (2), increased each consecutive week during the first quarter of 1986.

We can deduce the conclusion:

(4) The total quantity of good x demanded by all consumers of

good x, in the market defined in (2), decreased each consecutive week during the first quarter of 1986.

Thus our explanation of why the total quantity of good x demanded by all consumers of good x, in the given market, decreased each consecutive week during the first quarter of 1986, consists of demonstrating that this decrease in the demand for good x can be logically deduced from our simple theory (premise (1)) together with the initial conditions (premises (2) and (3)).

Note, however, that while this explanation involves *deductive reasoning* (which enabled us to reach the conclusion (4), given the premises (1), (2) and (3)), the primary emphasis in the inductivist procedure is essentially placed on observation and inductive reasoning. It is only after the simple theory of demand has been established by observation and inductive reasoning, and after the initial conditions have been established by observation, that deductive reasoning is introduced to demonstrate that if premises (1), (2) and (3) are true, then conclusion (4) is bound to be true.

Prediction in the inductivist procedure

Now that we have outlined explanation in the inductivist procedure, we can also briefly outline prediction in the inductivist procedure. To do this, let us assume that further observation and inductive reasoning has yielded the following universal statement about complementary goods (such as petrol and cars, or milk and breakfast cereals, which are consumed together):

(5) If goods m and n are complementary goods (with the symbols m and n referring to any pair of complementary goods), then the total quantity of good m demanded per week by all consumers of good m will increase (decrease) as the total quantity of good n demanded per week by all consumers of good n increases (decreases).

Also, let us assume that observation has established that:

(6) Good y, which is complementary to good x, may be bought and sold in the same market as good x.

With these two additional assumptions, plus our previous premises (1) and (2), we can now proceed to use deductive reasoning to obtain a prediction about the relationship between the demand for good y and the price of good x. Thus, given premises (1), (2), (5) and (6), we can logically deduce the following (as yet unobserved) prediction:

(7) If the price per unit of good x increases, then not only will the total quantity of good x demanded (per week by all consumers of good x in the market defined in (2)) decrease, but the total quantity of good y demanded (per week by all consumers of good y in the market defined in (2)) will also decrease.

The accuracy of this prediction can then be checked by observations of the relationship between the demand for good y and the price of good x.

As a final step, in our outline of the inductivist procedure, note that as the number of facts established by observation grows, so we progress to more and more theories of ever wider generality by inductive reasoning. Hence, as the stock of observation statements grows, so the ability to explain and predict grows.

2.2 SOME PROBLEMS FOR THE INDUCTIVIST

The inductivist procedure outlined above has an immediate attraction because of its apparent objectivity. Subjective opinion is apparently not permitted to intrude into either the process of observing (and recording) empirical facts or the process of inductive reasoning (known as *induction*) by which theories are derived from these facts.

Thus, in our investigation of consumer purchasing behaviour, it appears that we have started with reliable observations and then proceeded, via induction, to *prove* or *verify* that the total quantity of good x demanded per week by all consumers of good x is inversely related to the price per unit of good x. In other words, it appears that induction has enabled us to establish conclusively our simple theory of demand for good x (given by the universal statement (1) above) as true on the basis of the numerous (singular) observation statements. However, as we shall see below, there are several major difficulties which quickly destroy this seemingly favourable evaluation of the inductivist procedure.

How do we get from some to all?

The first major difficulty relates to the use of induction to establish conclusively the simple theory of demand for good x (given by the universal statement (1)) as true on the basis of the numerous (singular) observation statements. The difficulty here is simply that a universal statement cannot be logically derived from a number of singular statements. We cannot logically derive a statement that applies to *all* instances from statements (however many) that apply to *some* instances. Hence, in terms of the above example, this means that no number of (singular) observation statements would justify the claim that the (universal) theory of demand for good x is true. In other words, the only way we can move from (singular) observation statements to a (universal) theory of demand for good x is by making an illogical jump which takes us from some to all. Consequently, we have no guarantee that our theory of demand for good x (and thus any explanation based upon this theory) is true.

With regard to this first difficulty, it should be noted that it would not help matters even if we had somehow managed to observe reliably *all* instances of consumers purchasing good x in a certain period and, moreover, had found that in every instance the quantity of good x demanded was inversely related to the price of good x. While this situation would enable us to establish, via induction, our theory of demand for good x as true for this *particular period*, we could not conclude, via induction, that it is true for *all periods* without making an illogical jump.

Finally, with regard to this first difficulty, let us suppose that certain universal theories, derived by induction from observations, have not only been used on many past occasions, but also have always worked satisfactorily in the sense that no observations have contradicted these theories. Does this permit us to assert that the principle of induction is valid because it has been observed to work on a large number of past occasions? The answer is no. We cannot logically derive the universal statement that the principle of induction *always works* from a number of singular statements which indicate that applications of the principle of induction worked successfully on various past occasions. In other words, there is no guarantee that a theory, derived by induction from observations, which has worked satisfactorily in the past, will continue to work satisfactorily in the future.

How do we know what to observe?

A second major difficulty with the foregoing inductivist procedure relates to the belief that our investigation of consumer purchasing behaviour can start with pure observations alone. Thus, in our earlier discussion, it was stated that we simply go to a supermarket, where good x may be purchased, and start making observations without any preconceived notions as to the relative importance of the observed facts. But once we arrive at such a supermarket, *what* do we observe? To be instructed to go to such a supermarket and observe is meaningless—we need to know *what* to observe. Consequently, without this knowledge, the inductivist procedure cannot commence.

Yet if we decide to select certain observations (such as Q_{dx} and P_x) from among the infinite number of possible observations, then this means that we have *already* adopted a (simple) theory of consumer purchasing behaviour (namely, that Q_{dx} is related to P_x). Therefore our observation of facts will then be guided by this theory, rather than (as the foregoing inductivist procedure requires) the unprejudiced, unselective observation of facts guiding us to theory.

How do we know that observation statements are true?

A third major difficulty with the inductivist procedure relates to the belief that observation statements provide a reliable basis from which theories can be derived. Thus, throughout the foregoing discussion we simply regarded observation statements as true. But how do we know that observation statements are true? Is it possible to justify the claim that observation statements are true? Clearly this question of the validity or otherwise of observation statements is of utmost importance to the inductivist procedure. However, at this point, we shall merely note this difficulty and then return to examine it in more detail in Chapter 4.

2.3 THE INDUCTIVIST'S SOLUTION

Since the above three difficulties present serious problems for the inductivist, we shall now examine certain procedures which inductivists have utilized in an attempt to get around the first two difficulties. Note, in doing so, that we shall simply regard observation statements as true.

Hypothesis–led observation: from theory to observation

As noted above, the inductivist procedure faces the problem of not knowing *what* to observe. If, however, our investigation of consumer purchasing behaviour had started with a hypothesis (such as, for example, the hypothesis (or simple theory) that Q_{dx} is inversely related to P_x), then our observation of facts would have been guided by this hypothesis and, consequently, we would have avoided the problem of not knowing what to observe. For example, given the suggested hypothesis (and assuming that in all cases where two sets of events, such as the set of weekly demands for good x and the set of prices of good x, have a causal connection, the sets of figures providing appropriate measures of these events will be closely related to each other), we can readily move to the deduced consequence that observations of Q_{dx} will have a close inverse relation to observations of P_x.

The use of a hypothesis clearly solves the problem of what to observe, but it immediately raises the question of where such a hypothesis comes from. Could, for example, such a hypothesis be obtained by jumping from a few casual observations to a universal hypothesis? The answer is no, because even such casual observation must be guided by a hypothesis, otherwise the observer would not know which observations to select from among the infinite number of possible observations.

This leaves us in the position of recognizing that while economists are clearly capable of conceiving or inventing a hypothesis (or theory), it is by no means clear how they do so. In other words, the answer to the question of where such a hypothesis comes from appears to lie in the complex realm of the psychology of knowledge. However, the question of what are the mental processes by which a hypothesis is conceived need not concern us here. We shall simply accept that hypotheses can be conceived by economists. Also, we shall regard such hypotheses (or theories) as guesses or tentative conjectures, with these tentative conjectures being influenced by both a previous knowledge of the subject under study (consumer purchasing behaviour in our case) and an appreciation of the problems related to the study of this subject.

Now that we have a hypothesis, the next step is to make observations of Q_{dx} and P_x in order to see (or to test) whether or not our hypothesis is supported by the empirical evidence. Let us now suppose that we have taken this next step and have made these observations (which, by assumption, we shall regard as true). Also, let us further suppose that none of our (numerous) recorded observation statements conflict with our hypothesis. Does this now mean that we have empirically verified our simple hypothesis (or theory) of demand for good x? The answer is no. Our hypothesis (that Q_{dx} is inversely related to P_x) is a universal statement and, consequently, no number of singular observation statements would justify the claim that this universal statement is true. Thus, while the use of a hypothesis (or theory) removes the difficulty of what to observe, we still have no guarantee that the simple theory of demand for good x is true. Also, note that we have still simply assumed that our observation statements are true.

It is important to note that while numerous favourable observation reports cannot *verify* our hypothesis, only one contrary observation report (that is, one observation report stating, for example, that Q_{dx} *increased* as P_x increased) is required in order to *falsify* our hypothesis.

This immediately raises the question: do we intend our hypothesis to refer strictly to *all* cases (that is, to *all* consumers purchasing good x in *all* places at *all* times) or do we intend it to refer to *most* cases (that is, to *most* consumers purchasing good x in *most* places at *most* times)? If we intend our hypothesis to refer to most cases, then one contrary observation report would not falsify our hypothesis. For example, if we reformulate our hypothesis to state 'that, in not fewer than 99% of cases, Q_{dx} is inversely related to P_x', then we require contrary observations in more than 1% of the numerous cases observed before we can falsify the reformulated hypothesis.

Let us suppose that we are now working with the reformulated hypothesis. Also, let us suppose that numerous observations have failed to falsify this reformulated hypothesis. Does this mean that we have now verified the reformulated hypothesis? The answer is no. The fact that we have satisfied our 'in not less than 99% of cases' limit for the *particular* cases observed does *not* mean that we have satisfied this limit for *all* cases. As noted earlier, a universal statement cannot be logically derived from a number of singular statements.

Problems still remain

The question now arises: where does all this leave us? As noted above, the use of a hypothesis (or theory) will solve the problem of not knowing what to observe. But other problems still remain. Even if we use a hypothesis (and assume that we have reliable observations), we still cannot conclusively establish this (universal) hypothesis as true without jumping illogically from some to all. This means that while we have examined particular situations which would enable us to establish, via induction, our theory (or hypothesis) of demand for good x as true for a *particular period* or for *particular cases*, we have no guarantee that our simple theory (or hypothesis) of demand for good x is universally true. Hence, in turn, we have no guarantee that any explanation, referring to other periods or other cases, based upon this universal theory (or hypothesis) is true.

Faced with this difficulty, inductivists attempted to find a reasonable way round the verification problem by distinguishing between *verification* and *confirmation*.

2.4 CONFIRMATION RATHER THAN VERIFICATION

If we regard verification as the complete establishment of truth, then a universal theory (such as our simple theory of demand for good x) can never be verified (since no number of favourable singular observation statements can establish a universal theory as true). However, while we cannot verify a universal theory on the basis of favourable singular observation reports, inductivists have suggested that as the number of favourable observation reports grows (and assuming no contrary observation reports) our confidence in the theory will also grow. In other words, instead of talking about the *verification* of a theory, we can talk about the increasing *confirmation* of a theory. Hence, while we cannot speak of a universal theory being verified (or proved to be completely true) on the basis of favourable test outcomes, we can speak of the theory becoming more highly confirmed (or having a higher degree of confirmation relative to the available evidence) as the number of favourable test outcomes grows.

Once the notion of confirmability is accepted, this means that competing theories may then be appraised in terms of their relative degrees of confirmation. This, in turn, means that we then can choose among theories on the basis of their relative degrees of confirmation. In other words, the confirmationist will choose highly confirmed theories in preference to less highly confirmed and/or disconfirmed theories.

To aid our understanding of the confirmationist procedure, let us denote our simple (universal) theory of demand for good x (which relates Q_{dx} to P_x) as T_1. In addition, let us now suppose that a competing (universal) theory (which we shall denote as T_2) has also been proposed which relates Q_{dx} not only to P_x but also to the total income of all consumers of good x (which we shall denote as Y). Given this situation, note that since T_2 (relating Q_{dx} to P_x and Y) has more testable consequences than T_1 (which relates Q_{dx} to P_x only), then T_2 has potentially more explanatory content than T_1. Hence, if empirical tests empirically confirm this greater explanatory content, then T_2 is regarded as superior to T_1. In other words, if T_2 contains all the empirically confirmed consequences contained in T, plus some additional empirically confirmed consequences then T_2 is regarded as superior to T_1.

Is the most highly confirmed theory most likely to be true?
Note, in the foregoing example, that although T_2 is the most highly confirmed theory, confirmationists recognize that T_2 may not be true (since no number of favourable test outcomes can establish a universal theory as true). While this is so, we can now ask an interesting question: since T_2 is the most highly confirmed theory, does this mean that it is therefore the most probable? In other words, can we conclude that the more highly confirmed a universal theory is, the greater will be the probability that the theory is true (even though this high degree of empirical confirmation cannot guarantee that the theory is perfectly true)? At first sight, the answer would seem to be yes, since it appears intuitively correct to conclude that as the degree of empirical confirmation of a theory increases, the probability that it is true also increases. However, this intuition is not correct.

To see why this is so, note first that the probability of an event is measured by the ratio of the number of favourable outcomes to the overall number of possible outcomes. For example, let us suppose that an opaque bag contains ten identically sized balls, three of which are black and seven of which are red. If we now start to draw balls out of the bag, one at a time, then ten drawings will exhaust the total number of balls in the bag. Of these ten possible drawings, three are favourable to the drawing of a black ball. Hence, the probability of the first ball drawn out being black is 3/10.

The preceding paragraph implies that the probability of a (universal) theory being true will therefore be measured by the ratio of the number of favourable test outcomes to the overall number of possible outcomes claimed by the theory. Consequently, the probability of a universal theory being true must always be zero! Since a universal theory makes claims about an infinite number of possible outcomes, then the probability of a universal theory being true must always be a finite number (given by the number of favourable observation statements) divided by an infinite number and hence must always be zero. Moreover, this zero probability will still remain even if the number of favourable observation statements is vastly increased (since this vast number of favourable observation statements is still a finite number). Thus we must conclude that the probability of a highly confirmed universal theory being true is zero.

Clearly the above result, of not being able to assign a nonzero probability to a universal theory, leaves the confirmationist with an enormous difficulty. Not only is he unable to verify that a universal theory is completely true on the basis of favourable test outcomes, but also he is unable to conclude that as the degree of empirical confirmation of a universal theory increases the probability that it is true also increases.

Faced with this difficulty, confirmationists have introduced certain basic assumptions or presuppositions which, together with a finite number of confirming instances, enable them to assign nonzero probabilities to universal theories (for example, see Suppe [1977], pp. 624-32). The particular content of these presuppositions need not concern us here, other than to note that they generally imply that certain patterns of regularity are characteristic of the world. Rather, the important point to notice is that confirmationists have found it *necessary* to introduce certain presuppositions in order to conclude that the more highly confirmed a universal theory is the greater will be the probability that the theory is true. Clearly, however, if these presuppositions themselves cannot be established as true or probably true, then the confirmationist's problem remains. Thus, in trying to avoid one difficulty, the confirmationist has run into another difficulty.

The above discussion indicates that the inductivist's move from verification to confirmation has failed to reduce the problems associated with the inductivist procedure. Thus, in attempting to obtain a body of economic knowledge (or a set of universal theories) that can be established as true or probably true on the basis of empirical evidence, the inductivist procedure has run into one difficulty after another.

In addition, note that while inductivists have also argued that the inductivist procedure may well do better and cannot do worse than any noninductive procedure, it has been demonstrated that this claim is not always valid (see Watkins [1984] Chapter 3).

Note, however, that this does not mean that the inductivist procedure (in its confirmationist form) cannot be used. Rather, it means that the inductivist (or confirmationist) can only continue with his procedure in the hope that the most highly confirmed theory will be the most probable. Hence, when choosing among competing theories, the confirmationist will choose the most highly confirmed theory in the hope that it is most likely to be true. Similarly, with regard to the growth of economic knowledge, the confirmationist can only hope that as the body of economic knowledge grows via the accumulation of highly confirmed theories it will also improve its approximation to the truth.

The previous paragraph indicates that while the confirmationist can still use highly confirmed theories as a basis both for providing explanations of economic phenomena and for making economic policy recommendations, it must be remembered that he only does so in the hope that these underlying theories are most likely to be true.

However, faced with the above difficulty of obtaining a body of knowledge that is true or probably true on the basis of empirical evidence, and the absence of a generally-accepted, satisfactory resolution of this difficulty, other methodological procedures have been proposed. Consequently, in the following chapters, we shall proceed to an examination of some of these other methodological procedures.

Before we end this chapter with a short summary, we shall briefly note another problem which the inductivist procedure faces in common with various other methodological procedures.

A commensurability problem

This problem may arise in situations where we are attempting to appraise one theory T_2 as superior to another theory T_1. To appreciate this commensurability problem, note first that if T_2 contains all the empirically-confirmed explanatory content contained in T_1, plus some additional empirically-confirmed explanatory content not contained in T_1, then T_2 can be readily appraised as superior to T_1. In other words, in such a case, the superiority of T_2 to T_1 is defined in terms of a clear-cut gain in highly confirmed explanatory content. But what about the case where (1) T_2 contains some but not all of the empirically-confirmed explanatory content of T_1, and (2) T_2 contains an additional amount of empirically-confirmed explanatory content not contained in T_1? How are we going to compare T_1 and T_2 in such a case where both a loss as well as a gain in empirically-confirmed explanatory content is involved?

The answer to this question, as we shall see in later chapters, depends very much upon which philosopher of science we consult. Essentially we take the view (held by many philosophers of science and by many economists) that while there are difficulties in comparing the content and performance of competing theories, objective comparison of such theories can nonetheless still be made. In other words, we do not regard such theories as incommensurable (for support for this view, and for suggestions as to how the content-comparison problem can be solved, see Newton-Smith [1981], Chapter 7 and Watkins [1984], Chapter 5).

2.5 SUMMARY

In this chapter we have examined how the inductivist procedure may be utilized by economics researchers in an attempt to obtain a reliable, growing body of economic knowledge. In doing so, we have seen that the inductivist procedure essentially corresponds to the widely held 'common-sense' view that reliable knowledge is scientific knowledge which, in turn, is taken to be knowledge which has not only been rigorously derived from empirical evidence but which has also been objectively established as true on the basis of empirical evidence. However, as we have also seen, many difficulties have been encountered in attempting to achieve this goal of a reliable, growing body of knowledge.

One immediate difficulty is that it is not feasible for economics researchers to start by 'observing facts' and then be led by these facts into a general conclusion or theory about these facts. Rather, economics researchers need to know *what* to observe and this, in turn, presupposes that they already have a theory about the facts. Moreover, even if economics researchers have a theory, and even if we also assume that the relevant observation statements are true, the inductivist procedure does not enable economics researchers to establish this theory as true or probably true on the basis of these observation statements.

Consequently, inductivists have had to resort to introducing presuppositions in order to conclude that the most highly confirmed theory is most likely to be true. In other words, given these presuppositions, and assuming that the relevant observation statements are true, the inductivist proceeds in the hope that those theories which have the highest degree of empirical confirmation are most likely to be true. In this way, the inductivist economics researcher hopes that the body of economic knowledge will not only grow via the accumulation of highly confirmed theories but will also improve its approximation to the truth.

References for further reading

Discussion of inductivism can be found in Chalmers [1982], Chapters 1-3; Lakatos [1968b]; Popper [1972b], [1972c], and [1972d], pp. 3-59; Salmon [1975]; Stewart [1979], Chapter 3; Suppe [1977], pp. 624-32 and Watkins [1984], Chapter 3.

3 Instrumentalism

In Chapter 2 we examined some of the difficulties which inductivists must face when attempting to establish a theory or hypothesis as true or probably true on the basis of empirical evidence. Given these difficulties a pragmatic response might be simply to concentrate on those theories which predict well in relation to the empirical evidence. Since this response accords with the methodological procedure known as *instrumentalism*, which has enjoyed a certain popularity amongst economists, we shall now proceed to a brief examination of instrumentalism.

3.1 THE INSTRUMENTALIST PROCEDURE: THEORIES AS MERE INSTRUMENTS FOR MAKING PREDICTIONS

The first important point to note is that the instrumentalist does *not* concern himself with the problem of how a particular theory or hypothesis can be established as true or probably true. Rather the instrumentalist is only concerned with the *usefulness* of the conclusions or predictions that can be logically derived from a particular theory or hypothesis.

The instrumentalist sees a theory as merely an *instrument* for logically generating theoretical predictions. If these predictions are successful, in the sense that they are empirically confirmed when the theory is exposed to extensive empirical testing (with this testing proceeding on the assumption that the relevant observation statements are true), then the instrumentalist will accept this theory as a useful or adequate instrument for the task of generating these successful predictions. Whether the theory is true or false does not concern the instrumentalist. He is only interested in finding a convenient way of systematically generating successful predictions. Hence a theory (or hypothesis) is accepted simply because of its ability to generate successful predictions. In other words, the instrumentalist is not concerned with the truth status of a theory but rather with the practical usefulness or practical success of a theory. He does not attempt to prove that a theory is true, rather he simply argues that a theory should be accepted because of its ability to generate successful predictions.

An illustration of the instrumentalist procedure

In order to highlight the implications of the instrumentalist procedure, we shall now construct a deliberately artificial illustration of this procedure. To do this, we shall return to our illustration (introduced in Chapter 2) involving good x and introduce some further assumptions. First, let us assume that good x is a perishable good that is freshly supplied, by a single producer, to all supermarkets (in the market for good x as defined at the beginning of Chapter 2) on a weekly basis. Second, let us assume that the producer places certain prominent markings on good x to ensure that each new week's supply of good x can be readily distinguished from that of the previous week. Third, let us assume that this marking or coding system operates week by week for a thirteen-week (or one quarter year) period and then the whole scheme is repeated for the next quarter, and so on. For example, let us assume that the producer uses a coding scheme which involves stamping each unit of good x with two prominently-placed, adjoining coloured circles. In particular, let us assume that these two circles are coloured according to a rainbow-type sequence, so that the thirteen-week colour sequence is red and red, red and orange, orange and orange, orange and yellow, . . ., violet and violet.

Given this situation, let us now assume (as in Chapter 2) that Q_{dx} (the total quantity of good x demanded per week, in the given market, by all consumers of good x) decreased each consecutive week during the first quarter of 1986. Also, let us assume (for purpose of argument) that the true explanation of this weekly decrease in the demand for good x involves the inverse relation between Q_{dx} and P_x (the price per unit of good x). In other words, it is the consecutive weekly increases in P_x, during the first quarter of 1986, which provide the true explanation of the consecutive weekly decreases in Q_{dx} over the same period.

Let us further assume that, *prior* to this assumed background (i.e., *prior* to the first quarter of 1986), an instrumentalist economics researcher has already made the (rather unlikely) assumption that the demand for good x is related to certain colours. In particular, let us suppose that he has assumed that the demand for good x is related to the colour combination provided by the two coloured circles stamped on good x. This, in turn, has enabled him to formulate the following hypothesis: Q_{dx} is related to the colour combination provided by the two circles stamped on good x, with the relation being such that Q_{dx} will decrease as the colour combination of the two circles progresses (from red and red towards violet and violet) through the rainbow-type sequence.

Given this hypothesis, and assuming that the respective observation reports (of the quantities of good x demanded and of the pairs of coloured circles stamped on good x) provide appropriate measures of Q_{dx} and the colour combination of the two circles stamped on good x, the instrumentalist researcher is then able to move to the deduced conclusion or prediction that observations of Q_{dx} will be inversely related to observations of the position of the colour combination of the two circles in the rainbow-type sequence. Hence the instrumentalist's next step is to make the relevant observations in order to test whether or not this prediction is empirically successful.

Let us now suppose that the instrumentalist has taken this next step and that an extensive process of empirical testing, based on numerous observations made during the first quarter of 1986, has been completed. Also, let us suppose that this process of empirical testing has demonstrated that the instrumentalist's theoretical conclusion or prediction is successful in the specific sense that this prediction has been empirically confirmed by the tests made during the first quarter of 1986. Given this situation, the instrumentalist will now regard the 'colour' theory (or hypothesis) of demand for good x as an adequate theory (or hypothesis) for the task of successfully predicting the demand for good x over the first quarter of 1986. He is perfectly aware that he has not empirically verified the 'colour' theory of demand for good x, but this does not bother him. He is not concerned with trying to prove that this theory is true. He is only concerned with the practical success of the theory. Therefore, since the 'colour' theory of demand for good x has demonstrated its ability to generate successful predictions, the instrumentalist accepts it as adequate for the task of successfully predicting the demand for good x over the first quarter of 1986.

Successful prediction does not necessarily imply successful explanation

It is essential to note at this point, however, that successful *prediction* does not necessarily imply successful *explanation*. For example, in the foregoing illustration, we assumed that the true explanation of the consecutive weekly decrease in the demand for good x, during the first quarter of 1986, involves the inverse relation between Q_{dx} and P_x. This means that the genuine correlation will be between observations of Q_{dx} and observations of P_x over this period. In contrast, the instrumentalist's 'colour' theory involved the relation between Q_{dx} and certain colours which, in turn, gave rise to a spurious correlation between observations of Q_{dx} and observations of certain colours. Consequently, in the latter case, the successful prediction only reflects a spurious correlation rather than the genuine correlation associated with the true explanation. While the prediction has been successful in the sense that it is supported by the empirical evidence relating to the first quarter of 1986, this empirical success is simply due to the fact that the consecutive weekly increases in P_x (which were responsible for the consecutive weekly decreases in Q_{dx}) fortuitously coincided with the consecutive weekly changes in the colour coding on good x over the first quarter of 1986. Hence we can see how successful predictions may not imply successful explanation.

It is also important to note, however, that the instrumentalist need not be concerned about the fact that successful prediction may not imply successful explanation. The reason for this is simply that the instrumentalist economics researcher is only concerned with the predictive adequacy of a theory. In other words, prediction rather than explanation is the instrumentalist's goal. Consequently, since the above 'colour' theory has demonstrated its predictive accuracy, then the instrumentalist will still regard it as an adequate theory (for the task of successfully predicting the demand for good x over the first quarter of 1986) even though he is well aware that it may not be a true explanatory theory.

Any possible falsity of the assumptions is considered irrelevant

In order to enhance further our understanding of instrumentalism, let us further suppose that someone now criticizes the above 'colour' theory on the grounds that it may be based on a false assumption. For example, let us suppose that this critic is concerned that the assumption that Q_{dx} is related to certain colours may be counterfactual and, therefore, suggests to the instrumentalist that the factual accuracy of this assumption should be checked by additional empirical tests (such as tests involving observations of Q_{dx} when the coloured circles stamped on good x have been deliberately concealed).

Having introduced this criticism, note immediately that although such additional tests would clearly provide an important way of trying to ensure that the foregoing empirical relation between Q_{dx} and certain colours represents a genuine causal connection rather than a spurious correlation, the instrumentalist need not be concerned about responding to this criticism. For him the possibility of a false assumption is irrelevant. He simply wants a theory of demand for good x that is capable of generating successful predictions and he has now got one irrespective of the (claimed) false assumption.

Since the instrumentalist's 'colour' theory has successfully predicted an inverse relationship between observations of Q_{dx} and observations of the position of the colour combination of the two circles in the rainbow-type sequence, and since the observed inverse relationship can be considered to be a logical conclusion (prediction) from the argument containing the (claimed) false assumption, then the instrumentalist considers it quite acceptable to use this assumption. In other words, since the observed weekly decrease in Q_{dx}, during the first quarter of 1986, would have been the logical outcome if consumers of good x had actually behaved in accordance with the 'colour' theory over this period, then the instrumentalist can logically continue to claim that the observed weekly decrease in Q_{dx}, during the first quarter of 1986, is *as if* consumers of good x behaved in accordance with the 'colour' theory over this period. Hence, given that the instrumentalist's goal is prediction rather than explanation, he need not be concerned about any possible falsity of the assumptions in his theories as long as these theories meet his criterion of predictive adequacy.

(Although we have deliberately restricted the discussion of this sub-section to the simple demand theory illustration, it should be noted that the *as if* interpretation has been utilized to support the hypothesis of profit maximization in the theory of the firm (see Friedman [1953]) and the hypothesis of rational expectations in macroeconomics (see Begg [1982], Chapter 3 and Dow [1985], Chapter 6).)

The applicability of theories

Let us now suppose that not only have further empirical tests of the 'colour' theory been made during the *second* quarter of 1986, but also that these further tests have clearly indicated that the 'colour' theory's predictions are inconsistent with the empirical evidence relating to this period. Does this now mean that the instrumentalist regards his 'colour' theory as false? The answer is no. He is not concerned with whether his theory is true or false. He is only concerned with whether his theory is more adequate or less adequate for certain tasks. Thus the instrumentalist simply regards his 'colour' theory as adequate for the task of successfully predicting the demand for good x over the first quarter of 1986, but not adequate for the task of successfully predicting the demand for good x over the second quarter of 1986.

He does not regard his 'colour' theory as false, because of its inability to predict successfully the changes in demand for good x over the second quarter of 1986, rather he simply regards it as being applicable to the first quarter of 1986 but not applicable to the second quarter of 1986. In other words, rather than viewing the unsuccessful predictions as falsifying his 'colour' theory, the instrumentalist views them as an indicator of the 'colour' theory's limited applicability.

3.2 CRITICISM OF THE INSTRUMENTALIST PROCEDURE

As noted above, the instrumentalist is only concerned with the predictive adequacy of a theory. This, in turn, essentially means that the instrumentalist economics researcher views prediction rather than explanation as the goal of economics research. However, it is possible to take the view that economics research not only is but should be concerned with discovering theories which have explanatory power as well as predictive power. In other words, in contrast to the instrumentalist's view, it is possible to take the view that economics research should be concerned with gaining ever deeper understanding of the economic causes operating behind events so as to be able to provide ever fuller explanations of these events. Consequently, if the latter view is taken, instrumentalism should then be rejected as an unsatisfactory methodological procedure for economics, since it disregards the explanatory content of theories by regarding them as nothing more than instruments for prediction.

If it is accepted that economics research is concerned with explanation as well as prediction, then the major thrust of economics research should be directed towards the discovery of true, explanatory theories. In contrast to this, instrumentalism allows economics researchers to abandon the search for such theories. Rather than urging economics researchers to pursue a critical methodological procedure, and to strive for the growth of economic knowledge, it permits them to be complacent. For example, as we have already seen, instrumentalism's lack of concern about the possible falsity of assumptions leads to the complacent acceptance of (predictively adequate) theories rather than to the rigorous and extensive testing of theories. Clearly, if one is concerned with explanation as well as prediction, this is a most serious shortcoming. To be content with high correlation, rather than continuously searching for ever fuller explanation of economic phenomena, is most unsatisfactory.

Moreover, if it is accepted that economics research is concerned with obtaining a reliable, growing body of economic knowledge, instrumentalism can be seen to have additional shortcomings. For example, let us suppose that theory T_1 provides both a causal explanation and a prediction of some economic event. In contrast, let us also suppose that while theory T_2 provides a prediction of this same event it does not provide a causal explanation. Given this situation, note that the strict application of instrumentalism would lead economics researchers to prefer T_2 over T_1 if T_2 provides a better prediction of the economic event than T_1. But this immediately raises a problem. If the explanatory content of theories is neglected in this way, how then can economics researchers adequately assess the growth of economic knowledge?

In addition, while it may be difficult to assess whether a theory is true or false (or partly true and partly false), it can be claimed that a theory nonetheless *is* either true or false (or partly true and partly false) in virtue of how the economic situation under investigation is in actuality. Hence if we ignore the whole issue of the truth status of theories, as the instrumentalist does, then we cannot talk about growth in the body of economic knowledge in the sense that the historically generated sequence of theories is improving its approximation to the truth. Moreover, if unsuccessful predictions are only regarded as an indicator of the limited applicability of a theory, rather than as falsifying counterinstances, then this means that we cannot adequately distinguish between better and worse theories and hence we cannot assess the growth of economic knowledge.

Confronted with these strong criticisms of instrumentalism, we shall proceed (in Chapter 4) to an examination of another methodological procedure, known as *falsificationism*, which has been proposed in an attempt to overcome the difficulties associated with both inductivism and instrumentalism.

3.3 SUMMARY

Faced with the difficulties encountered by inductivists in attempting to establish a theory or hypothesis as true or probably true on the basis of empirical evidence, the instrumentalist has responded to these difficulties by proposing a methodological procedure which deliberately ignores the whole issue of the truth of theories. Thus, as we have seen, the instrumentalist is not concerned with whether a theory is true or false. Rather the instrumentalist simply views theories as *nothing more* than instruments for logically generating theoretical predictions. If these predictions are (empirically) successful, then the instrumentalist regards the theories which generated them as adequate instruments for the task of generating these successful predictions.

While the instrumentalist procedure has an evident attraction due to its preoccupation with the practical usefulness or success of a theory, it has nonetheless been strongly criticized as an unsatisfactory methodological procedure for economics. As noted above, the main criticism is directed towards its neglect of the explanatory power of theories. This neglect, as we have seen, makes it difficult to distinguish between better and worse theories and, in turn, to assess the growth of economic knowledge. In addition, instrumentalism has been criticized on the grounds that instead of urging economics researchers to pursue a critical methodological procedure, and to strive for ever fuller explanations of economic phenomena, it permits the complacent acceptance of mere correlation and so retards the growth of economic knowledge.

References for further reading

As the economics Nobel laureate Milton Friedman is an influential instrumentalist, students should read Friedman [1953]. For further discussion of instrumentalism and economics, students will find Boland [1979]; Caldwell [1982], pp 51-3, 173-88 and Wong [1973] particularly helpful.

For material written from a philosophy of science viewpoint, see Giedymin [1976]; Newton-Smith [1981], Chapter 2; Popper [1972d], Chapter 3 and Wisdom [1987a], Chapter 3.

4 Falsificationism

In Chapter 3 we concluded that instrumentalism represented a rather unsatisfactory response to the problems associated with inductivism. An alternative, and in many ways more satisfactory, response to the problems associated with inductivism is the falsificationist procedure proposed by the philosopher Karl Popper. Since the falsificationist procedure attempts to overcome the difficulties associated with both the inductivist and the instrumentalist methodological procedures, we shall now proceed to a detailed examination of falsificationism.

Theories not viewed as true or probably true

The falsificationist explicitly recognizes that a universal theory (or hypothesis) cannot be logically derived from a number of singular observation statements. The falsificationist is therefore adamant in stressing that no number of singular observation statements would logically justify the claim that a given universal theory was true. He specifically recognizes that, even if we assume that we have numerous true observation statements, the only way we can move from such singular observation statements to a universal theory is by making an illogical jump which takes us from some to all. Hence the falsificationist explicitly accepts that a theory cannot be inductively established as true.

In addition, the falsificationist explicitly accepts that one cannot say that a highly confirmed universal theory is more probable, or more likely to be true, since (as we noted in Chapter 2) the probability of a universal theory being true is zero. Thus, faced with the inductivist's difficulty of obtaining a growing body of knowledge that is true or probably true on the basis of empirical evidence, and rejecting the instrumentalist procedure as unsatisfactory, the falsificationist has proposed (as we shall see below) an alternative methodological procedure.

Theories viewed as tentative conjectures

The falsificationist also explicitly recognizes that observation must be guided by a theory or by an hypothesis, otherwise the observer would not know what to observe. This immediately raises the question of where such a 'prior to detailed observation' theory or hypothesis comes from. Could, for example, such a theory or hypothesis be obtained by jumping from a few casual observations to a universal theory or hypothesis? The falsificationist's answer is no, because even such casual observation logically presupposes a guiding theory or hypothesis. Rather, the falsificationist regards theories or hypotheses as having been conceived or invented by an economist (via a mental process that, at present, is not adequately understood) in an attempt to explain some state of affairs. Consequently, the falsificationist economics researcher views such mentally-derived theories or hypotheses as *tentative conjectures* or tentative solutions to certain economic problems.

4.1 THE FALSIFICATIONIST PROCEDURE: ONLY THE FITTEST THEORIES SURVIVE

In order to explain further the falsificationist's viewpoint, let us now suppose (with reference to the assumed problem, given at the beginning of Chapter 2, of the consecutive weekly decreases in the demand for good x, in the given market, during the first quarter of 1986) that we have got a universal theory or hypothesis. For example, let us suppose that an economist has tentatively conjectured that Q_{dx} is inversely related to P_x.

Now that we have a simple theory of demand for good x, how do we proceed? Is there some empirical procedure which will enable us to establish conclusively our theory of demand for good x as true? The falsificationist's answer is no, because no number of favourable observation reports (indicating an inverse relationship between observations of Q_{dx} and observations of P_x) could logically establish our simple theory of demand for good x as true. However, while numerous favourable observation reports do not enable us to *verify* logically our universal theory, only one contrary observation report (for example, one observation report stating that Q_{dx} *increased* as P_x increased) will enable us to *falsify* or *refute* our universal theory logically. As we shall see, it is exactly this logical point that the falsificationist procedure utilizes.

The falsificationist procedure essentially consists of taking a tentative theory, such as our theory of demand for good x, and exposing it to extremely rigorous empirical testing with a view to falsifying (rather than *verifying*) it. For example, our simple theory of demand for good x could be rigorously tested by obtaining numerous observations of Q_{dx} and P_x under as many different conditions as possible. If this theory is eventually falsified as a result of such rigorous testing, then it is rejected and replaced by another tentative theory. This new theory is, in turn, exposed to rigorous and extensive empirical testing with a view to falsifying it. When this new theory is likewise falsified after some period of extensive testing, the whole procedure of tentative conjecture followed by rigorous empirical testing and eventual falsification (or refutation) is repeated over and over again.

The essential thesis behind the falsificationist procedure is that we can learn from our mistakes. The falsificationist thus conjectures that in finding out that a tentative theory is false we have got nearer the truth.

In other words, the falsificationist conjectures that economic knowledge progresses via the trial and error sequence involved in the continuous process of proposing tentative theories and falsifying them. Since, in this process, falsified theories are eliminated and replaced by other tentative theories, then only the fittest theories survive. Consequently, a currently unfalsified theory is regarded as superior to its predecessors in the sense that it has not only been able to pass the rigorous empirical tests that its predecessors passed but it has also been able to withstand the rigorous empirical tests that falsified its predecessors. Hence, while we can never say that this currently unfalsified theory is true (because further tests may eventually lead to its falsification), the falsificationist conjectures that this theory is a better approximation to the truth than its predecessors.

Note, in the foregoing outline of the falsificationist procedure, that the overthrow of theories is regarded as the vehicle of scientific progress. Hence the refutation of a theory will not only largely determine the choice of problem economics researchers work on, but will also lead to the proposal of replacement theories. In other words, empirical refutations are regarded as the essential driving force leading to the proposal of new theories and hence to the growth of economic knowledge.

An illustration of the falsificationist procedure

In order to enhance our understanding of the above procedure, let us assume that we have started a rigorous test of the tentative theory (introduced in our discussion of instrumentalism in Chapter 3) that Q_{dx} is related to certain colours. Also, let us assume that while initial tests (conducted during the first quarter of 1986 and involving both observations of Q_{dx} and observations of certain colours) have failed to falsify this theory, additional tests (involving observations of Q_{dx} when the colour coding on good x is concealed) have falsified this theory by indicating that Q_{dx} can change irrespective of the colour coding on good x. Now that this theory has been falsified, the next step in the falsificationist procedure is to propose another tentative theory.

As an example, let us suppose that an economist has proposed that Q_{dx} is inversely related to P_x. This new theory would then, in turn, be exposed to rigorous empirical testing. Whenever it is also eventually falsified, other tentative theories of demand for good x would likewise be proposed and tested. In this way progress would hopefully be made to increasingly superior theories which, for example, may relate Q_{dx} not only to P_x but also to the prices of other goods (denoted as P_i) and the total income of all consumers of good x (denoted as Y).

In order to appreciate more fully what is meant by one theory being superior to another, note that since the latter theory (denoted as T_2) relating Q_{dx} to P_x, P_i and Y, has more testable consequences than the former theory (denoted as T_1) which related Q_{dx} to P_x only, then T_2 has potentially more explanatory content than T_1. Moreover, note that T_2 can be subjected to more rigorous empirical tests than T_1 (in the sense that T_2 can be subjected to tests not only involving the relation between Q_{dx} and P_x but also involving the relation between Q_{dx} and P_i and the relation between Q_{dx} and Y).

Thus, for example, when we come to test T_2 empirically we may find that (a) T_2 has not only passed those tests which T_1 has passed but also T_2 has passed tests which T_1 has failed, and (b) T_2 has not only suggested tests additional to those suggested by T_1 but also T_2 has passed these additional tests. In such a case, T_2 is regarded as superior to T_1. Hence, in the falsificationist account, T_2 is regarded as superior to T_1 if

(1) T_2 is more falsifiable (or more severely testable) than T_1, and
(2) T_2 has survived more severe testing than has T_1.

Note, in relation to the preceding paragraph, that the falsificationist does not regard the currently unfalsified T_2 as true (because further empirical tests may lead to its eventual falsification). Rather, he conjectures that T_2 constitutes a better approximation to the truth (or corresponds better to the facts) than T_1.

4.2 VERISIMILITUDE AND CORROBORATION

In order to appreciate exactly what the falsificationist means by the last sentence of the preceding paragraph, note that the basic idea underlying the falsificationist's notion of approximation to truth (or of *truthlikeness* or of *verisimilitude*) is that T_2 is better than T_1 if

(1) T_2 contains more true consequences than T_1, and
(2) T_2 contains fewer false consequences than T_1.

But this, however, immediately raises an interesting question: can the falsificationist measure the degree of verisimilitude of a theory, given his view that a theory cannot be established as true on the basis of empirical evidence? The falsificationist's answer is no. However, while the falsificationist cannot provide a measure of the *actual* verisimilitude of a theory, he has suggested a measure (known as the *degree of corroboration* of a theory) which can be taken as an indication of how a theory's verisimilitude *appears*, at a point in time, in comparison with another theory (or with other theories).

The *degree of corroboration* of a theory is taken to be a report describing, at a point in time, how well an unfalsified (but falsifiable) theory has stood up to empirical tests. In other words, the degree of corroboration of a theory is essentially a measure of the severity of the empirical tests it has passed. For example, let us suppose that theory T_1 has been proposed and then severely tested over some period. Further, let us suppose that T_1 has successfully withstood these tests and, consequently, has been given a degree of corroboration. In addition to this, let us suppose that a competing theory T_2, which contains all the testable consequences contained in T_1 plus some additional testable consequences not contained in T_1, has also been proposed and severely tested without refutation over the same period. Given this situation, T_2 will be given a higher degree of corroboration than T_1 (since T_2 has withstood more severe tests than T_1).

Note, however, that the respective degrees of corroboration of T_1 and T_2 do not measure the *actual* verisimilitude of T_1 and T_2 at that point in time. Rather, the falsificationist takes these respective degrees of corroboration as an indication of the *apparent* verisimilitude of T_1 and T_2 at that point in time. In other words, the falsificationist regards the degrees of corroboration as a guide to the preference between T_1 and T_2 at that point in time. Thus, the higher degree of corroboration of T_2 (compared to that of T_1 at that point in time) is viewed as telling us that T_2 *seems* nearer to the truth than T_1 and this, in turn, is viewed as a rational basis for preferring T_2 to T_1, at that point in time.

Also note, in relation to the above discussion, that falsificationists do not regard theories as true because they are highly corroborated. In addition, note that falsificationists do not regard T_2 as more probable than T_1 because T_2 has a higher degree of corroboration than T_1. (Recall, in contrast to this, how the inductivist regards T_2 as more probable than T_1 because T_2 has a higher degree of confirmation than T_1.) Moreover, since the degree of corroboration is a report evaluating the *past* performance of a theory, the falsificationist explicitly regards the degree of corroboration of a theory as saying nothing whatsoever about the *future* performance or reliability of a theory.

Corroboration and the growth of knowledge

Let us now suppose that further tests have falsified T_1 but not T_2. Clearly, in this situation, the falsificationist will still prefer theory T_2, which has withstood these further tests, to theory T_1 which has failed these tests. But what if yet further tests falsify T_2? Can we still say that T_2 is a better theory than T_1, even though both have now been shown to be false? The falsificationist's answer is yes. Since T_2 has withstood tests which T_1 did not pass, this is taken as an indication that T_2 (even after its falsification) *appears* to be a better approximation to the truth than T_1.

Let us further suppose that not only has another theory T_3 now been proposed but also that it has withstood all the tests which have falsified its predecessors T_1 and T_2. Clearly, since T_3 seems to be a better approximation to the truth than T_1 and T_2, falsificationists will prefer T_3 to its predecessors. If T_3 is eventually joined by other highly corroborated theories which are also unfalsified (but falsifiable), then the body of knowledge in this particular area of economics can be viewed as growing via this accumulation of theories.

If a similar accumulation of unfalsified theories takes place in other areas of economics, then the overall body of economic knowledge can also be viewed as growing. Moreover, not only is the overall body of economic knowledge viewed as growing in such a situation, but (given that the theories constituting this body of knowledge are viewed as having more apparent verisimilitude than their falsified predecessors) it also appears that this growing body of knowledge is gradually improving its approximation to the truth.

Obviously it is hoped that the growing body of knowledge is not only gradually improving its *apparent* approximation to the truth, but is also gradually improving its *actual* approximation to the truth. However, according to the falsificationist, there is no guarantee that this is so. As we have seen, the falsificationist argues that there is no way of establishing that actual (rather than apparent) convergence towards the truth is taking place.

The falsificationist maintains that at best we can only claim that there is every indication that the current body of knowledge (or set of highly corroborated, unfalsified theories) is the best approximation to the truth. Note, however, that while this claim may be less than we would like it to be, it does nonetheless provide an objective reason for basing explanations and predictions on these highly corroborated, unfalsified (but falsifiable) theories.

Falsifiability, explanatory content and improbability

Finally, before leaving this section, note that if theory T_2 contains all the testable consequences contained in theory T_1, plus some additional testable consequences not contained in T_1, then T_2 has potentially more explanatory content than T_1. Also, note, in this situation, that T_2 is more falsifiable or more severely testable than T_1. In other words, since T_2 can be subjected to more severe tests than T_1, this means that T_2 has more potential falsifiers (or is more improbable, or runs a greater risk of being false) than T_1. Thus higher content means higher falsifiability and, at the same time, lower probability.

Hence, whereas the inductivist recommends selecting (from among competing, unfalsified theories) the *most probable* theory, the falsificationist recommends selecting the *most falsifiable* theory. This, in turn, means that the falsificationist recommends selecting the *more improbable* theory. Note, however, that if the highly falsifiable theory thus selected survives severe testing to become highly corroborated then (although it is not regarded as true or more probable) the falsificationist would claim that there is every indication that this theory constitutes a considerable improvement in the body of knowledge's approximation to the truth. Consequently, such highly falsifiable, highly corroborated theories will be highly preferred for future testing as a means of further improving the apparent verisimilitude of the body of knowledge (even though their high degrees of corroboration are viewed as saying nothing whatever about the *future* performance or reliability of these theories).

4.3 SOME PROBLEMS FOR THE FALSIFICATIONIST

Now that we have provided an introduction to the falsificationist procedure, we can proceed to a more detailed consideration of falsificationism. To do this, we shall first introduce certain problems for the falsificationist in this section and then examine the falsificationist's proposals for dealing with these problems in the next section.

As a starting point, recall (from earlier discussion) that while numerous favourable observation statements do not logically enable us to verify a given universal theory, only one contrary observation statement will logically enable us to falsify this universal theory. In particular, note that if this one contrary observation statement is *true*, then we can *conclusively* falsify the given universal theory. But this immediately raises a difficult problem: how can we prove that this contrary observation statement is true? Clearly, if we cannot be certain that any given observation statement is true, then conclusive falsification is impossible. This, in turn, means that we cannot apply the falsificationist procedure in the manner outlined above.

Fallible, theory-impregnated observation statements

The falsificationist is not only well aware of the above problem, but also explicitly claims that we cannot prove that a given observation statement is true. In other words, he explicitly recognizes that observation statements are *fallible*.

Moreover, in addition to this, the falsificationist also explicitly recognizes the *theory-dependence* of observation statements. For example, when it comes to making observations of the colour coding on good x (in connection with the theory of demand for good x, introduced in Chapter 3, which related Q_{dx} to certain colours), the falsificationist recognizes that this presupposes a universal theory of colours (which guides our observations of particular colours). In other words, the falsificationist accepts that observation statements are not completely independent of theory. Rather, he accepts that they are *theory-impregnated*. Consequently, since we cannot verify a given universal theory, then the theory-dependence of observation statements implies that we cannot verify given observation statements either.

The Duhem problem

In addition to the problem of fallible, theory-impregnated observation statements, the falsificationist must face a further problem, known (after the physicist Pierre Duhem) as the *Duhem problem*, which arises from the complexity of the empirical testing process (even when we ignore the problem of fallible observation statements).

To appreciate this problem, note that the empirical testing of a simple theory or hypothesis of demand for good x, such as that which related Q_{dx} inversely with P_x, involves not only the collection of numerous observations of Q_{dx} and P_x, but also the analysis of these observations to see whether or not they indicate an inverse relationship between Q_{dx} and P_x. In practice this analysis of observations is usually made with the aid of statistical techniques which are capable not only of demonstrating whether or not an inverse relationship exists between Q_{dx} and P_x, but also of demonstrating whether or not the observations of Q_{dx} and P_x are closely related.

However, while the use of statistical techniques is standard practice in test situations, it is important to note that such techniques have been derived from statistical hypotheses or theories which, in turn, contain universal statements. This means that whenever we carry out an empirical test we are not just testing our original hypothesis, but rather the original hypothesis together with all these statistical hypotheses (with the latter supportive hypotheses being known as *auxiliary hypotheses*). This, in turn, complicates the whole process of falsification. For example, if empirical tests fail to indicate a close inverse relationship between Q_{dx} and P_x, does this necessarily mean that our original hypothesis is false? Logically it does not. Rather, it may well be one or more of the auxiliary hypotheses which is false.

To complicate matters further, it should be noted that our original hypothesis will usually contain a *ceteris paribus* clause. For example, when considering the relation between Q_{dx} and P_x, it is often specifically assumed that the prices of other goods, consumers' incomes, and consumers' tastes are constant. Note that this means that the relation between Q_{dx} and P_x is therefore always being considered together with other hypotheses—in this case, the three particular hypotheses('there is no change in the prices of other goods', 'there is no change in consumers' incomes' and 'there is no change in consumers' tastes') embedded in the *ceteris paribus* clause. Consequently, when empirical tests fail to indicate a close inverse relationship between Q_{dx} and P_x, it may well be one of the hypotheses embedded in the *ceteris paribus* clause which is false rather than our original hypothesis.

Moreover, when it is remembered that the *ceteris paribus* clause is designed not only to exclude changes in the prices of other goods, consumers' incomes, and consumers' tastes, but also to exclude a potentially infinite number of other changes (such as war, strikes, government intervention, advertising, etc.), then an awareness of this (plus an awareness of the earlier point about auxiliary hypotheses) indicates that no individual hypothesis can be conclusively falsified. Since we are always testing a particular hypothesis together with numerous other hypotheses, then we can never be sure that we have falsified the particular hypothesis itself.

The commensurability problem

Lastly, as a further problem for the falsificationist, we shall note a particular difficulty that arises when we are attempting to appraise one theory T_2 as better than its predecessor T_1. In doing so, recall that we have been appraising T_2 as superior to T_1 if T_2 both contains more empirically testable consequences than T_1 and has survived more severe empirical tests than T_1. Note, however, in making this appraisal, that we have been essentially referring to the situation where T_2 contains all the empirically-corroborated explanatory content contained in T_1, plus some additional empirically-corroborated explanatory content not contained in T_1. In other words, we have been essentially referring to the situation where the shift from T_1 to T_2 involves a clear-cut gain in explanatory content.

But what about the situation where (1) T_2 contains some, but not all, of the empirically-corroborated explanatory content of T_1, and (2) T_2 contains an additional amount of empirically-corroborated explanatory content not contained in T_1? How are we going to compare T_1 and T_2 in such situations where both a loss as well as a gain in empirically-corroborated explanatory content is involved?

4.4 THE FALSIFICATIONIST'S SOLUTION

Faced with the above problems, the falsificationist proposes that we should adopt certain methodological rules which will help us to overcome these problems in the most objective and most rigorous manner possible.

Intersubjectivity

With regard to fallible observation statements, the falsificationist proposes that economists should simply agree to accept observation statements for falsifying purposes, with the important proviso that this acceptance is as objective and as rigorous as possible. For the falsificationist this means that economists should only agree to accept observation statements that have themselves survived rigorous attempts at falsification. Also, it means that economists should only accept such rigorously tested observation statements when they can readily agree (and check) that these tests are as rigorous as it is possible for them to be in the current state of development of economics. Note, however, that such agreement (known as *intersubjectivity*) does *not* mean that observation statements are accepted as true. Rather, the acceptance is tentative since these accepted observation statements are still regarded as fallible.

Reproducible falsification

In addition to the above methodological rule, the falsificationist proposes that a few contrary observation statements should *not* instantly falsify a theory. Rather, he proposes that a theory should only be regarded as falsified when it can be rigorously demonstrated that the falsifying observation statements can be readily *reproduced* under clearly specified test conditions. This means that a theory will therefore be protected from the danger of premature rejection and, consequently, from the danger of being discarded before its contribution to economic knowledge has been adequately evaluated.

Ad hoc modifications forbidden

While on the one hand the falsificationist does not want to encourage economists to reject a theory prematurely, on the other hand he does not want to encourage them to cling to a theory any longer than is necessary. In particular, he wants to avoid the situation where a theory is modified merely in order to protect it from threatening falsification. This means, for example, that he wants to avoid modifications such as the changing of the *ceteris paribus* clause (or the changing of the auxiliary hypotheses, or the changing of the existing assumptions of the theory) which are merely designed to save a theory from threatening falsification.

Since the adoption of several such modifications (known as *ad hoc* modifications) could completely immunize a theory from falsification, the falsificationist proposes that *ad hoc* modifications should never be used to save a theory from falsification. Instead, he proposes only the adoption of those modifications which will *increase* (rather than decrease) the degree of testability or falsifiability of such a threatened theory. Clearly, since such modifications to a theory would lead to new tests, and therefore to increased risk of falsification, then the non-falsification of this modified theory (in the face of these new tests) means that we have learnt something new and hence our economic knowledge will have grown. In contrast, the adoption of *ad hoc* modifications would make the modified theory less falsifiable (and thus less testable) than the original theory and, consequently, would retard the growth of economic knowledge.

As an example of an *ad hoc* modification, note that our simple theory of demand (which related Q_{dx} inversely to P_x) could be immunized from any threatening falsification by an *ad hoc* modification such as 'Q_{dx} is not only related to P_x but is also related to consumers' unconscious psychological impulses'. This *ad hoc* modification permits *any* consumer behaviour (related to the purchase of good x) not explained by the (inverse) relation between Q_{dx} and P_x to be explained by these unconscious impulses. Consequently, the modified theory is less testable than the original theory. This is due to the fact that we not only cannot readily obtain empirical measures of these unconscious impulses but we also cannot now readily test the relation between Q_{dx} and P_x without the possibility that (unknown to us) the empirical relation is being reinforced, offset or unaffected by these unconscious impulses. Moreover, the modified theory cannot be falsified since any pattern of consumer purchasing behaviour is consistent with this modified theory.

In contrast, the non-*ad hoc* modification 'Q_{dx} is not only related to P_x but is also related to the prices of certain other goods (namely, those goods which are substitutes for or complements to good x) and to consumers' incomes' will increase the degree of testability or falsifiability of our theory of demand because it leads to new (or novel) testable predictions, which do not follow from our original (falsified) theory of demand (which related Q_{dx} to P_x only).

Response to the Duhem problem

The falsificationist recognizes, along with Duhem, that since a particular hypothesis is always being tested together with numerous auxiliary hypotheses and a *ceteris paribus* clause, then the source of any falsification may be located in one or more of the auxiliary hypotheses, and/or the *ceteris paribus* clause, rather than in the particular hypothesis itself. Also, he recognizes that he can never be sure just which part of this complex test situation is responsible for the refutation.

Consequently, to deal with this problem, the falsificationist proposes the following two-step procedure. First, *tentatively* accept the auxiliary hypotheses and the *ceteris paribus* clause as unproblematic background knowledge and proceed to test the particular hypothesis in question. Second, if the foregoing tests appear to falsify the particular hypothesis, then check the auxiliary hypotheses and the *ceteris paribus* clause. If the latter check fails to falsify the auxiliary hypotheses and the *ceteris paribus* clause, then the particular hypothesis is regarded as responsible for the initial refutation and is therefore regarded as falsified.

The falsificationist is well aware that the foregoing two-step procedure does not completely avoid the Duhemian difficulty. In particular, he recognizes the difficulty of checking a *ceteris paribus* clause severely. Consequently, he recognizes that his two-step procedure is risky in the sense that it may result in a given hypothesis or theory being erroneously regarded as falsified when the source of the falsification is actually located in the *ceteris paribus* clause. However, the falsificationist is willing to accept this risk (which essentially means that the given hypothesis or theory is permitted to bear the brunt of empirical tests) because he feels that this risky procedure will not only encourage a critical (rather than a defensive) attitude, but will also encourage the growth of economic knowledge.

The incommensurability thesis rejected

Leaving the Duhem problem and turning to the problem of comparing theories when both a loss as well as a gain in empirically-corroborated explanatory content is involved, let us briefly note that while falsificationists accept that there are difficulties in comparing the content of such theories, they argue that objective comparison of such theories can nonetheless still be made. In other words, falsificationists explicitly reject the thesis that such theories are incommensurable. (For a suggested solution to the content-comparison problem, see Watkins [1984], Chapter 5.)

Preference for bold conjectures

Finally, the falsificationist also proposes that new theories, which are put forward as replacements for falsified theories, should take the form of bold, highly falsifiable conjectures. These bold, risky conjectures should then, in turn, be subjected to the most severe empirical tests in a rigorous attempt to falsify them. Since we would expect such risky conjectures or theories to be readily falsified, then, if these theories survive this severe testing to become highly corroborated, this means that there is every indication that these theories represent a considerable improvement in the body of knowledge's approximation to the truth.

Consequently, such theories can be regarded as better than their predecessors because they have not only led to additional new tests and therefore to more severe testing, but also because they have so far passed these more severe tests and therefore appear to constitute a better approximation to the truth than their predecessors. In other words, there is every indication that these unfalsified, risky theories represent an important advance in economic knowledge. Thus, as we noted earlier in the chapter, it is for this reason that falsificationists have a preference for bold theories that are highly falsifiable (or severely testable).

If these bold theories repeatedly survive rigorous attempts at falsification, then the falsificationist not only regards them as highly corroborated but also conjectures that this accumulation of highly corroborated theories constitutes a considerable improvement in the growing body of knowledge's approximation to the truth.

Before ending this chapter with a brief summary, note that we have deliberately excluded certain criticisms of falsificationism from this chapter. These criticisms will, however, be examined in subsequent chapters. Thus, in Chapters 5, 9 and 10, we shall see how falsificationism can be criticized as inadequate on historical grounds. Also, in Chapter 7, we shall see how falsificationism can be criticized in terms of the practical difficulties encountered in implementing the falsificationist procedure in economics.

Finally, note that while Popper held that the aim of science is to progress towards the truth with theories that are ever better approximations to the truth (or have an ever higher degree of verisimilitude), with preference for the best corroborated theory (at each relevant point in time) being taken as the methodological means towards this aim, Popper's analysis of verisimilitude and of the link between corroboration and verisimilitude has been heavily criticized (for example, see Newton-Smith [1981], Chapter 3). Despite this, many philosophers still accept that increasing verisimilitude should be taken as the aim of science, provided a more adequate analysis of verisimilitude can be found (see Watkins [1984], p.280).

(For an attempt to provide such an analysis, by bringing in an inductivist strategy, see Newton-Smith [1981], Chapters 8 and 9. For a completely different analysis which (although it involves the idea of truth) does not use the notion of approximation to truth or verisimilitude in outlining the optimum aim for science, deliberately avoids any inductivist strategy, and proposes preference for better corroborated theories, see Watkins [1984].)

4.5 SUMMARY

Faced with the inductivist's difficulty of obtaining a growing body of knowledge that is true or probably true on the basis of empirical evidence, and rejecting the instrumentalist methodological procedure as unsatisfactory, the philosopher Karl Popper proposed an alternative methodological procedure known as falsificationism.

As noted above, the essential thesis underlying the falsificationist procedure (which, as we have already seen, consists of the falsifiability principle *plus* certain methodological rules) is that we can learn from our mistakes. Thus, the first stage of the falsificationist procedure consists of theories being put forward (by economics researchers) as conjectures or as tentative solutions to economic problems. The second stage then involves the rigorous testing of these theories. This rigorous testing, however, is aimed at the *falsification* of these theories rather than at their verification or confirmation. The reason for this emphasis on refutation is that the falsificationist views the refutation of a theory as a most important way of increasing our understanding of the problem under consideration. In other words, the falsificationist views the refutation of a theory as a step which takes us nearer to the truth.

The falsificationist therefore regards refutations, or the overthrow of theories, as the vehicle of scientific progress. Refutations of theories thus not only largely determine the choice of problem economics researchers work on, but also lead to the proposal of replacement theories. In other words, empirical refutations are regarded as the essential driving force leading to the proposal of new theories and hence to the growth of economic knowledge.

As also noted above, theories that are currently unfalsified, despite having been subjected to rigorous testing, are each given a degree of corroboration. This degree of corroboration measures the severity of the empirical tests that the respective theory has passed. However, while currently unfalsified theories may be highly corroborated,it is important to note that falsificationists do not regard such theories as true because they are highly corroborated. Rather, the falsificationist only takes the respective degrees of corroboration as an indication of the *apparent* (rather than the *actual*) verisimilitude of these theories.

In addition, the falsificationist uses the respective degrees of corroboration as a guide to the preference between competing theories at a point in time. Note, however, that this does not mean that falsificationists regard one theory T_2 as more probable than another theory T_1 because T_2 has a higher degree of corroboration than T_1. Rather, T_2's higher degree of corroboration is viewed as telling us that T_2 *seems* nearer to the truth than T_1 and this, in turn, is taken as a rational basis for preferring T_2 to T_1 at that point in time.

Finally, as the body of economic knowledge grows via the accumulation of highly corroborated, unfalsified (but falsifiable) theories, the falsificationist claims that, at any point in time, there is every indication that the current body of economic knowledge is the best approximation to the truth. In other words, since the theories constituting this body of knowledge are viewed as having more apparent verisimilitude than their falsified predecessors, it appears that this growing body of economic knowledge is gradually improving its approximation to the truth. Thus, while the falsificationist argues that there is no way of establishing that actual (rather than apparent) convergence towards the truth is taking place, he claims that the falsificationist procedure does nonetheless provide an objective reason for basing explanations and predictions on the current set of highly corroborated, unfalsified (but falsifiable) theories.

References for further reading

Popper's falsificationism (first published in German in 1934) is presented in Popper [1959] and further developed in Popper [1972a] and [1972d].

Discussion and criticism of falsificationism can be found in Ackermann [1976]; Blaug [1980a], pp 10-28, and [1985]; Caldwell [1982], pp. 41-5; Chalmers [1982], Chapters 4-6; Hands [1985a]; Harding [1976]; Koertge [1975] and [1979b]; Lakatos [1970] and [1971a]; Musgrave [1973]; O'Hear [1980]; Radnitzky [1976]; Schilpp [1974]; Watkins [1978] and Wisdom [1987a].

5 From Falsificationism to Lakatosian Research Programmes

In this chapter we shall first present certain criticisms of the falsificationist methodology and then proceed to introduce yet another methodology, known as the *methodology of scientific research programmes,* which attempts to overcome these criticisms. This introduction to the methodology of scientific research programmes, with its economic illustration of a research programme, will then be followed by a more detailed exposition of this methodology in Chapter 6.

5.1 CRITICISMS OF FALSIFICATIONISM

In our earlier discussion of falsificationism, we noted that the falsificationist views the growth of economic knowledge as the outcome of a series of conjectures and refutations. Thus, while the truth of any particular theory is not certain, and while the convergence of successive theories towards the truth is not certain either, the falsificationist procedure is specifically designed to try to ensure that only the fittest theories survive and, therefore, to ensure that, at any point in time, there is every indication that the current body of economic knowledge is the best approximation to the truth. As such, it should be noted that falsificationism is *prescriptive* in the sense that it aims at providing economists with advice on how to proceed so as to promote the growth of economic knowledge. It does not attempt to provide a *description* of how economists actually proceeded in the past.

While it is important to note this distinction between *prescription* and *description*, the very mention of the actual practice of economists immediately gives rise to the interesting question: does an examination of the actual practice of economists provide us with any useful insight as to the adequacy or otherwise of falsificationism? The answer is yes. For example, if periods of substantial growth in economic knowledge were characterized by widespread utilization of the falsificationist procedure, then this would constitute important support for the adoption of falsificationism. Contrariwise, if descriptive studies indicate that economics researchers often proceed in a non-falsificationist way, and if there is a significant methodological rationale for doing so, then this may be taken as a criticism of falsificationism. In other words, the descriptive adequacy or otherwise of falsificationism is important to its evaluation.

Before we make any reference to the actual practice of economists, let us first highlight certain features of the falsificationist account that will be relevant to our immediate discussion. Thus, let us recall that the falsificationist account envisages a theory (T_1) being conceived and then being subjected to empirical tests. When T_1 is eventually falsified then another theory (T_2) is conceived and, in turn, empirically tested. Provided T_2 contains more empirically testable consequences or predictions than T_1, and provided that T_2 has successfully withstood more severe empirical tests than T_1, then T_2 is regarded as superior to T_1 (we shall ignore here the content-comparison problem and simply assume that the shift from T_1 to T_2 involves only a clear-cut gain in explanatory content).

Although the falsificationist account does not regard the currently non-falsified T_2 as true, it views T_2 as having every indication that it is a better approximation to the truth than T_1. Eventually, however, T_2 may be falsified and another theory (T_3) will then be proposed and the whole procedure repeated. In this way it is envisaged that economics research will progress to apparently superior theories (T_1, T_2, T_3, . . .) and hence the growth of economic knowledge will be promoted.

Most theories are born refuted

Note, in the above falsificationist account, that each of the theories T_1, T_2, T_3, . . . was essentially regarded as having been conceived or *born unrefuted*. In other words, refutation is only viewed as taking place *after* empirical testing. Unfortunately, however, this does not accord with the history of economics. Rather, in practice, most theories are *born refuted* in the sense that they were inconsistent with certain well-known empirical evidence when first proposed. Hence it is not uncommon for an economist to propose a theory even though he knows in advance that this theory will be inconsistent with certain empirical results which are already widely available.

As we shall see, such a situation has serious implications for falsificationism. However, before noting these implications, let us first enhance our understanding of this situation by reference to a simple, contrived, illustration. To do this, let us suppose that for the last 100 years a careful record has been kept of the total quantity of good x demanded per week (denoted by Q_{dx}). Also, let us suppose that not only is this data series widely available but also that it is well known that throughout the third quarter of one particular year the figures for Q_{dx} were uncharacteristically low. In particular, let us assume that Q_{dx} was zero throughout this specific quarter. Moreover, let us assume that since no unusual changes took place in certain other variables (such as the price per unit of good x, the prices of other goods, or consumers' incomes) during this specific quarter, no satisfactory explanation of this anomaly has yet been provided.

Now that we have constructed this background, let us think of an economist proposing a simple theory (T_1) of demand for good x. For example, let us suppose that he proposes that Q_{dx} is inversely related to the price per unit of good x (denoted by P_x). Note, in proposing this theory, that the economist is fully aware that it is inconsistent with the existing empirical evidence (in the sense that he already knows that there is no inverse relation between Q_{dx} and P_x during the anomalous quarter). In other words, T_1 is born refuted. If another theory (T_2) of demand for good x is now proposed, suggesting that not only is Q_{dx} inversely related to P_x but also that Q_{dx} is positively related to consumers' incomes (denoted by Y), then T_2 is also born refuted (in the same sense that the existing empirical evidence shows that Q_{dx} has neither an inverse relation to P_x nor a positive relation to Y during the anomalous quarter).

Such a situation, which is not uncommon in the history of economics, clearly raises serious problems for falsificationism. For example, if the history of economics not only shows that both T_1 and T_2 were born refuted but also shows that T_2 is widely regarded as vastly superior to T_1, then how does falsificationism account for this situation? The answer is that it cannot.

To see why this is so, recall (from Chapter 4) that the falsificationist takes the degree of corroboration of a theory to be a report describing, at a point in time, how well a non-falsified (but falsifiable) theory has stood up to empirical tests. Also, recall that the falsificationist takes the respective degrees of corroboration of two theories such as T_1 and T_2 as an indication of the *apparent* verisimilitude of T_1 and T_2 at that point in time. In other words, the falsificationist regards the degrees of corroboration as a guide to the preference between T_1 and T_2 at that point in time.

Now that we have recalled this aspect of falsificationism, let us proceed to see what happens if we introduce the assumption that both T_1 and T_2 were born refuted. For example, let us now assume that both T_1 and T_2 were refuted by certain empirical evidence (such as the anomalous quarter mentioned above) when first proposed. Also, let us assume that both T_1 and T_2 remained refuted by this anomaly until they were replaced by other theories. Given these assumptions, note immediately that in such a situation *both* T_1 and T_2 would have the lowest possible degree of corroboration *throughout* the whole period from conception to replacement. This, in turn, means that the falsificationist cannot explain economics researchers' preference for T_2 over T_1 in terms of the degrees of corroboration (or apparent closeness to the truth) of T_1 and T_2. Consequently, since most theories are born refuted by being born into a sea of anomalies (though, see Watkins [1984], Chapter 8), falsificationism can be criticized as inadequate in this respect.

Refutations often ignored in practice

Moreover, not only have economists proceeded to use theories which have been born refuted but they have also, for certain periods, tenaciously held on to particular theories even though they were well aware that certain falsifications or refutations had arisen at some stage in the life of these theories. While falsificationism may permit a certain amount of such behaviour so as to avoid the premature rejection of a theory, it clearly does not want to encourage excessive tenaciousness in the face of falsifying evidence. Consequently, falsificationism must regard such tenacious behaviour as irrational. This, however, means that if economics researchers do in fact have a sensible rationale for such behaviour, then such behaviour (which is by no means uncommon in the history of economics) provides additional grounds for criticizing falsificationism as inadequate.

Finally, with regard to actual practice, it should be noted that economics research is often characterized by numerous theoretical developments which are accompanied by both a relatively small amount of empirical testing and a relatively low regard for empirical refutations. To the extent that there is an important rationale for this situation, then this also provides further grounds for criticizing falsificationism as inadequate.

The need for another methodology

The above criticisms of falsificationism, based on an examination of the actual practice of economists, indicates the need for a methodology which can explain (1) why certain falsifying evidence (for example, such as the evidence which accounted for T_1 being born refuted or certain falsifying evidence which may arise at a later stage in the life of T_1) is often ignored (at least initially) and (2) why one theory may be regarded as superior to its predecessor even though both these theories were born refuted.

To be more exact, note that (2) above implies that we need a methodology that enables us to appraise *groupings of hypotheses*. To see why this is so, recall (from our earlier discussion of the Duhem problem in Chapter 4) that a theory or hypothesis (such at T_1 or T_2 above) is always being tested together with numerous other hypotheses. Thus, instead of considering T_1 individually, we are actually considering a particular grouping of hypotheses. Likewise, instead of considering T_2 individually, we are actually considering another grouping of hypotheses. In other words, an examination of actual practice indicates that, instead of considering a temporal sequence of *individual* theories or hypotheses, we are always considering a temporal sequence of *groupings* of hypotheses. Consequently, we need a methodology that will explain why one grouping of hypotheses is preferred to another.

Since the *methodology of scientific research programmes* is specifically concerned with the problem of appraising groupings of hypotheses, we shall now proceed to an examination of this methodology.

5.2 THE METHODOLOGY OF SCIENTIFIC RESEARCH PROGRAMMES : THEORIES AS PRODUCTS OF A RESEARCH PROGRAMME

The methodology of scientific research programmes (which is denoted as MSRP for short) was initially developed by the late philosopher of science Imre Lakatos, and subsequently extended by others, in an attempt to overcome the criticisms directed against falsificationism.

To aid our understanding of MSRP, let us think of a group of economists investigating certain problems (such as the problems related to the efficient allocation of resources) in the field of microeconomics. Given such a situation, it is unlikely that we would expect the researchers involved to be proceeding in a completely arbitrary fashion. Rather, we would expect them to have a fairly definite research strategy or *research programme* that provides guidance for their current and future investigations. In other words, we would expect these researchers to be involved in a fairly definite 'microeconomics research programme' which provides at least some guidance both as to how they should proceed and as to how they should not proceed. It is exactly this *programmatic* aspect of research activity, with its associated positive and negative guidance for future research, that MSRP both recognizes and incorporates into methodological appraisals.

If we now define a *Lakatosian research programme* as a framework or structure that provides both positive and negative guidance for future research, we can then proceed to a more detailed examination of the component parts of such a research programme.

The negative heuristic of a research programme

The part of a Lakatosian research programme which provides guidance as to how not to proceed, or what paths of research to avoid, is known as the *negative heuristic* of the programme. Essentially the negative heuristic of a research programme amounts to the requirement that the basic assumptions or fundamental hypotheses underlying the programme, which Lakatos calls the *hard core* of the programme, are not to be exposed to falsification. In other words, the negative heuristic of a research programme is the methodological rule which stipulates that the hard core of the programme must not be rejected or modified during the development of the programme.

To enhance our understanding of the negative heuristic and the hard core of a research programme, let us return to the foregoing 'microeconomics research programme' (which is both a well-established and well-documented ongoing research programme in economics) for a specific illustration of these new terms.

5.3 THE HARD CORE OF THE MICROECONOMICS RESEARCH PROGRAMME

In our view, the hard core of the class of theories constituting microeconomics (as *predominantly* taught in western universities, polytechnics and schools) essentially consists of the following basic assumptions or hypotheses:

Individualism: It is assumed or hypothesized that microeconomic analysis will rest on propositions about *individual* behaviour, with the individual economic agent being conceived in abstraction from his social and historical setting. Essentially this means that the microeconomic analysis of any situation will always begin with the behaviour of individual economic agents (such as individual consumers, individual workers or individual entrepreneurs), with this behaviour being analysed in an asocial and ahistorical manner.

In addition to placing the emphasis on the behaviour of individuals, it is also assumed that each individual economic agent is only motivated by self-interest. In other words, each agent is envisaged as pursuing his own welfare without taking account of the welfare of others (whether 'others' refers to certain persons or to society in general).

Rationality: It is assumed or hypothesized that the behaviour of each economic agent is *rational*. Essentially this assumption embodies the requirement that agents make their economic calculations in a consistent way. Hence, given a particular problem-situation, rational behaviour is viewed as that behaviour which is appropriate to this given situation in the sense that each economic agent acts in a way that is consistent with his given preferences. When taken in conjunction with the assumption of individualism, this means that the consistent behaviour of economic agents is exclusively related to the preferences of individuals, with the characterization of these preferences being independent of the individual economic agent's social and historical setting. Thus, if an individual's preference ordering is represented by a utility function, then he chooses rationally when he chooses what he prefers, or when he chooses so as to maximize utility.

(While the notion of rationality given in the text is that which is commonly used in orthodox economic analysis, it should be noted that the concept of rationality has been the subject of considerable discussion (e.g., see Hahn and Hollis [1979]). Also, note that Lawson [1985] argues that orthodox economic analysis has neglected Keynes's viewpoint in which the behaviour of individual economic agents and the social situation interact with each other so as to give rational behaviour both a social and a historical dimension.)

Private property rights: Individual economic agents are assumed or hypothesized to have two kinds of *property rights*. The first kind relates both to the individual agent's mental and physical abilities and to his own labour time, while the second kind relates both to some amount of goods and services that either have been produced or will be produced and to some amount of natural resources (such as rivers, forests, or land).

With regard to the first kind of property right, each individual agent is assumed to have a private ownership right over his own body and over his own labour time. With regard to the second kind of property right, each individual agent is assumed to have a private ownership right over some *unspecified* amount of goods and services and natural resources. (Since a property right over services may not be so obvious as a property right over goods, let us think of a consumer purchasing a freezer. In such a case, the consumer may not only purchase the freezer itself but may also purchase a freezer insurance policy. To the extent that the latter policy entitles the consumer to future freezer repairs and maintenance, then this consumer has a property right over these future freezer repair and maintenance services.)

It is important to note, with regard to the second kind of property right, that no *particular* initial ownership of goods and services and natural resources is being assumed for each individual agent. In other words, while microeconomic analysis assumes that individual agents have a property right over themselves and over their own labour time it does not assume a particular initial distribution of ownership over goods and services and natural resources. Rather microeconomic analysis permits *any* initial distribution of ownership over goods and services and natural resources.

It is also important to note that, in addition to the above assumptions about property rights, it is assumed that no individual should violate another individual's property rights. Consequently, it is also assumed that the individual's property rights are protected (for example, it could be assumed that the legal system of a country provides protection against the violation of property rights resulting from aggressive behaviour originating within the country, and that the government of that country provides protection against the violation of property rights resulting from aggressive behaviour originating outside the country).

Market economy: The rational behaviour of individual economic agents is assumed or hypothesized to take place in a *market economy*. An essential characteristic of such an economy, in contrast to an economy where the decision-making is centralized and collective, is that the market economy permits decentralized decision-making by individual citizens. Consequently, in a market economy, economic agents (with their respective property rights in terms of labour time and in terms of goods, services and natural resources) are characterized as taking individual decisions with regard to the buying and selling of goods, services, natural resources and labour time. Each individual economic agent is thus characterized as coming to the market, with his respective property rights, to make individual decisions in the pursuit of his own self-interest without violating other people's property rights.

The hypotheses listed under the above four headings represent, in our view, the basic hypotheses underlying the (predominant or orthodox) research programme in microeconomics. As such, this 'hard core' of hypotheses forms the basis from which (orthodox) microeconomic analysis is to develop.

5.4 THE NEGATIVE HEURISTIC OF THE MICROECONOMICS RESEARCH PROGRAMME

Now that we have outlined the hard core of the microeconomics research programme, the negative heuristic of this programme can readily be seen to be the *methodological rule* which stipulates that the specific group of hypotheses constituting the hard core of the microeconomics research programme is not to be exposed to falsification. In other words, the negative heuristic of this programme requires that during the development of the programme the hard core is to remain unmodified and intact.

In practical terms, the implementation of this methodological rule essentially involves the isolation of certain hypotheses which are not only accepted by convention (or by agreement, with this agreement usually being implicit) but are also regarded as irrefutable by the participants in the microeconomics research programme. In other words, the group of hypotheses constituting the hard core of the microeconomics research programme is rendered 'hard' or 'inflexible' by the *methodological decision* of the adherents to this programme. Since a discussion of the rationale for this methodological decision presupposes knowledge of other component parts of a Lakatosian research programme, we shall postpone this discussion until later.

The positive heuristic of a research programme

The part of a Lakatosian research programme which provides guidance as to how to proceed, or what paths of research to pursue, is known as the *positive heuristic* of the programme. Essentially the positive heuristic of a research programme consists of a set of rough guidelines indicating how that programme might be developed. In other words, the positive heuristic provides a set of suggestions as to how the hard core of the programme is to be supplemented in order for the programme to be capable of providing explanations and predictions of the phenomena under consideration. As such, the positive heuristic guides the production of specific theories within the programme, with each specific theory not only being *constructed around* the programme's hard core but also *implying* that hard core (see Worrall [1978a], p.59). Also, in addition to guiding the production of specific theories within the programme, the positive heuristic provides guidance as to how to proceed when difficulties arise in the development of the programme.

To enhance our understanding of the positive heuristic of a research programme, let us return once more to the foregoing microeconomics research programme for a specific illustration of this new term.

5.5 THE POSITIVE HEURISTIC OF THE MICROECONOMICS RESEARCH PROGRAMME: GUIDELINES FOR THE PRODUCTION OF SPECIFIC THEORIES WITHIN THE PROGRAMME

As noted above, the positive heuristic guides the production of specific theories within a research programme. Thus, within the microeconomics research programme, the positive heuristic would consist of guidelines such as:

(1) Divide the respective markets for goods, services, natural resources and labour into buyers and sellers. In other words, the microeconomic analysis of the allocation of goods, services, natural resources and labour is to proceed in terms of *demand and supply*.
(2) Specify the *market structure*. For example, a perfectly competitive market structure may be assumed. Under this assumption the number of buyers and sellers in a given market is assumed to be large enough so that no one of them has any appreciable influence on price. In other words, individual economic agents are assumed to be price-takers.
(3) Assume that each economic agent has *complete information* about the relevant features of his decision-making situation so as to eliminate uncertainty.
(4) Specify *goals* for individual economic agents. For example, individual consumers are usually assumed to have the goal of utility maximization, while individual producers are usually assumed to have the goal of profit maximization.
(5) Specify the *constraints* that each economic agent faces in his decision-making situation. For example, each consumer is usually assumed to be making consumption decisions, with a view to maximizing utility, subject to the constraints of his given income and the given prices of goods. Similarly, each producer is usually

assumed to be making production decisions, with a view to maximizing profit, subject to the constraints of his given technology (or his given production function which shows how output produced is related to the amounts of inputs employed) and the given prices of output and inputs.

(6) Specify what is embodied in the relevant *ceteris paribus* clauses. For example, in relation to consumption decisions the *ceteris paribus* clause may require that consumers' tastes remain constant over the relevant period. To the extent to which age, religion, ethnic culture, etc., determine the tastes of consumers, then these in turn are also assumed to remain constant over the relevant period. Also, for example, it may be assumed that the quality of goods is constant over the relevant period and that there is no advertising of goods. In relation to the production decision, the *ceteris paribus* clause may require that there is no technological change over the relevant period. Also, it may require that there are no strikes and no government interference over the relevant period.

It should be noted, in relation to the *ceteris paribus* clauses, that while certain hypotheses such as 'tastes are constant', 'there is no technological change' may be clearly specified, the *ceteris paribus* clauses will contain many other unspecified hypotheses such as 'there is no civil war', 'there is no influenza epidemic', etc. In other words, the *ceteris paribus* clauses are designed to exclude a potentially infinite number of changes in the relevant economic situation.

(7) Analyse the economic situation under consideration using the analytical techniques of *optimization* or *determination of equilibrium*, whichever is appropriate to the given situation.

For example, in the analysis of consumer decision-making, the technique of *optimization* involves finding the combination of goods which, if bought, would maximize the consumer's utility subject to his limited income and the given prices of goods. Having done this, the next stage in the analysis of the consumer's optimum is to examine how this optimum varies in response to changes in the constraints. Thus, for example, we may examine how the consumer's optimum varies in response to (a) an increase in his limited income, with the prices of goods held constant, and (b) a fall in the price of one good (say, good x), with the consumer's income and the price of other good (in the two-good case) held constant. (Also, in case (b), it is usual to separate the 'income effect of the price change' from the 'substitution effect of the price change'.)

Since (b) enables us to see how the quantity demanded of good x varies with changes in the price of good x, this means that we can plot the individual consumer's 'demand curve' for good x. If we do this for each individual consumer, then we shall know how much each individual consumer demands of good x at each price of good x. Hence, by summing up these quantities over all individuals, we can obtain the aggregate quantity demanded, by all consumers of good x together, at each price of good x. This, in turn, means that we can then plot the 'aggregate or market demand curve' for good x.

While the above analytical techniques of optimization subject to constraints, variation of the optimum by changing the constraints, and the obtaining of aggregate or market results may be quite familiar from the elementary theory of consumer choice, it should be noted that they are widely used in microeconomic analysis in general. In other words, they are an essential part of the positive heuristic of the microeconomics research programme. Also, it should be noted that when the positive heuristic proposes the use of optimization analysis this, in turn, implies both the use and development of appropriate mathematical techniques for analysing optimization problems.

For an example of analysis involving the *determination of equilibrium*, we shall only recall the demand-supply analysis which is presented in almost all introductory microeconomics textbooks. In such textbooks the determination of equilibrium is usually presented graphically, with the equilibrium (or balance of demand and supply in the market) being represented graphically by the price-quantity point where the market demand and supply curves intersect. Moreover, as should be familiar, the assertion that the intersection of the market demand and supply curves is an equilibrium (or state of balance) is supported by the following two hypotheses:

(a) an excess of quantity demanded over quantity supplied (arising, graphically, when the market price is momentarily at some level lower than the equilibrium price) is assumed to lead to an increase in price,

(b) an excess of quantity supplied over quantity demanded (arising, graphically, when the market price is momentarily at some level higher than the equilibrium price) is assumed to lead to fall in price.

The next stage in the analysis of equilibrium problems involves the method of *comparative statics*. This method of analysis involves displacing the initial equilibrium in a given market by introducing certain changes which shift either the initial demand curve or the initial supply curve (or both initial curves) and then obtaining the new or final equilibrium position as given by the intersection of the 'post-shift' demand and supply curves. Having done this, we can then compare the initial and final equilibrium situations. Thus, with reference to the standard demand-supply diagrams, we may for example generate a rightward shift in the market demand curve for a good by introducing an increase in the level of consumers' incomes. Likewise, we may for example generate a rightward shift in the market supply curve for a good by introducing an important technological invention.

(Finally, before leaving this brief discussion of equilibrium analysis, it should be noted that more advanced analysis also involves an investigation of the path that the market follows when moving from the initial to the final equilibrium. The latter form of analysis is known as *dynamic analysis*.)

Once more, while the above techniques of equilibrium analysis (involving mainly the determination of equilibrium followed by comparative-static analysis) may be quite familiar from the elementary theory of demand-supply analysis, it should be noted that they are widely used in microeconomic analysis in general. In other words, they are an essential part of the positive heuristic of the microeconomics research programme. Also, it should be noted that when the positive heuristic proposes the use of equilibrium analysis this, in turn, implies both the use and development of appropriate mathematical techniques for analysing equilibrium problems.

(8) Analyse the economic situation under consideration by constructing *a series of ever more complicated theories*. In other words, the analysis is to commence with theories which are deliberate simplifications of reality. Subsequently, as the research programme develops, these idealizations are to be replaced by increasingly sophisticated and hopefully more realistic theories. For example, in the elementary theory of the firm there is no separation between ownership and control of the firm. Rather the decision-maker is simply taken to be the entrepreneur who is represented as both owning and controlling the firm. However, in a more sophisticated theory of the firm, it is desirable to take

account of the fact that ownership (by shareholders) is not only often separated from control (by hired managers) but also may involve a conflict of interest (between shareholders and managers) in certain situations.

The above list of guidelines should be sufficient to illustrate how the positive heuristic of the microeconomics research programme guides the production of specific theories within that programme. In providing this illustration, it is important to note that the above guidelines involve a set of hypotheses (such as 'the market is perfectly competitive', 'economic agents have complete information', 'firms have the goal of profit maximization', . . ., plus the numerous hypotheses underlying the *ceteris paribus* clauses) which is distinct from the set of hypotheses constituting the hard core of the microeconomics research programme. This additional set of hypotheses constitutes what is termed the *protective belt* of the microeconomics research programme. (The rationale behind this terminology will become clear as we proceed).

5.6 THE POSITIVE HEURISTIC OF THE MICROECONOMICS RESEARCH PROGRAMME: GUIDELINES FOR COPING WITH DIFFICULTIES IN THE DEVELOPMENT OF THE PROGRAMME

So far we have only indicated how the positive heuristic of the microeconomics research programme guides the production of specific theories within that programme. Now we must also indicate how the positive heuristic of the microeconomics research programme provides guidance as to how to proceed when difficulties arise in the development of the programme.

To help us understand this further aspect of the positive heuristic of the microeconomics research programme, let us refer to the elementary theory of the firm which presents the producer as a price-taker (meaning that he can greatly increase or diminish his output without affecting the market price significantly). In relation to this theory, let us suppose that empirical work has provided observations which are contrary to those predicted by the theory. In particular, let us suppose that the anomalous empirical observations indicate that variations in the producer's output do influence the market price significantly.

Now that a difficulty has arisen in relation to a particular part of the microeconomics research programme, how are we to respond to this difficulty? Clearly we cannot respond to this situation by regarding the hard core hypotheses (which are implied by the theory of the firm) as falsified, given that the negative heuristic requires that these hypotheses are not to be exposed to falsification. Rather the hard core hypotheses are to remain unmodified and intact despite this difficulty. So how are we to proceed?

The answer provided by the positive heuristic is that the *protective belt hypotheses* are to be modified so as to accommodate the anomaly. Thus, for example, instead of assuming or hypothesizing that the producer is a price-taker, it may now be assumed or hypothesized that the producer can influence the market price by varying his output (that is, by reducing his output he can push the market price up and by increasing his output he can push the market price down).

Note that this modification is not an *ad hoc* modification (see Section 4.4), since this modification can readily be tested. Also note that since the protective belt hypotheses are modified in response to the challenge presented by the anomalous empirical observations, this means that the hard core hypotheses are 'protected' from challenge. This explains why the former hypotheses are termed the protective belt of the research programme. Finally, it should be noted that such modifications of the protective belt hypotheses will result in specific new theories being constructed or produced in accordance with the guidance provided by the positive heuristic of the research programme as to how to respond to empirical difficulties.

Moreover, in relation to the question of how to proceed in the presence of anomalous empirical observations, it should be noted that the positive heuristic may also suggest that in some cases the best available response may be simply to take note of the anomaly and then shelve it for future consideration. In other words, in some cases it may be best to proceed with the research programme, ignoring the anomaly for the present time, in the hope that it can be accommodated (by some non-*ad hoc* modification of the protective belt) at a later stage of development of the programme.

It is important to note that the discussion of the preceding paragraph also relates to the situation of a theory being born refuted. In such a situation, the positive heuristic advice is simply to proceed to use the theory within the research programme, ignoring (for the present time) the empirical evidence which was responsible for the theory being born refuted. This advice is given in the hope that, at a later stage of development of the programme, it will be possible to accommodate this anomaly by some non-*ad hoc* modification of the protective belt. In other words, the positive heuristic enables economics researchers to set aside various anomalies as problems to be dealt with at a later date rather than regarding them as counterinstances falsifying either the entire research programme or certain theories within it.

Finally, it should be noted that the positive heuristic also provides guidance as to how to proceed when logical (as opposed to empirical) difficulties are encountered in the development of a research programme. Thus, when logical difficulties or inconsistencies arise in the development of a research programme, the positive heuristic provides guidelines or suggestions as to how these problems may be resolved via certain non-*ad hoc* modifications of the protective belt hypotheses.

Since we have covered quite a lot of new ground, we shall end this chapter with a brief summary of the foregoing discussion of a Lakatosian research programme. Before doing so, note that in Chapter 6 we shall provide a more detailed exposition of the methodology of scientific research programmes. Also, note that in Chapter 8 we shall provide more comprehensive examples of research programmes in economics. As we shall see in Chapter 8, one of these examples involves re-classifying the microeconomics research programme as something less than a full Lakatosian research programme. However, as will be explained in Chapter 8, this re-classification of the microeconomics research programme does not affect the validity of the foregoing discussion (essentially because the more comprehensive research programme introduced in Chapter 8 not only has the same hard core as the microeconomics research programme but also incorporates the latter's positive heuristic within a somewhat larger positive heuristic).

5.7 SUMMARY

Economics researchers (for example, in the field of microeconomics) are not viewed as proceeding in an arbitrary fashion, but rather are viewed as being involved in a fairly definite research *programme* which provides them with guidance both as to how they should proceed and as to how they should not proceed. Consequently, a research programme is envisaged as containing two major methodological rules: one (the *negative heuristic*) telling researchers what paths of research to avoid and the other (the *positive heuristic*) telling researchers what paths of research to pursue.

A research programme is composed of two groups of hypotheses. One group (the *hard core*) contains the basic assumptions or fundamental hypotheses underlying the research programme and is protected (by methodological decision) from empirical falsification. Hence when a research programme faced empirical refutations its hard core hypotheses are not to be modified or replaced. Rather they are deemed irrefutable by methodological decision. The other group of hypotheses (the *protective belt*) protects the hard core hypotheses in the sense that it (rather than the hard core) is to be modified or replaced when the research programme is challenged by empirical refutations and/or logical difficulties.

References for further reading

Lakatos's methodology of scientific research programmes is presented in Lakatos [1970] and further elaborated in Lakatos [1971a] and [1971b]. Further references on MSRP are given at the end of Chapters 6, 7 and 8.

6 Lakatos's Methodology of Scientific Research Programmes

Now that the component parts of a Lakatosian research programme have been examined in Chapter 5, we can proceed to a more detailed exposition of the *methodology of scientific research programmes* (denoted as MSRP for short). In particular, we shall now outline MSRP's proposals for appraising the historical development of a research programme.

6.1 APPRAISING THE HISTORICAL DEVELOPMENT OF A RESEARCH PROGRAMME

In commencing our discussion of the historical development of a research programme, note immediately that the positive heuristic is regarded as being the major driving force underlying the development of a research programme. To appreciate this point, recall that the positive heuristic of a programme consists of a set of rough guidelines indicating how the programme might be developed. Consequently, the positive heuristic functions as the major driving force underlying the development of a research programme by guiding the production of specific theories within the programme. Hence, as the suggestions or instructions laid down in the positive heuristic are followed, specific theories will be constructed to supplement the hard core of the programme and thus the programme will develop over time.

For examples of how the positive heuristic of the foregoing microeconomics research programme (introduced in Chapter 5) has guided the production of specific theories, which not only incorporate the analytical techniques of either optimization and/or equilibrium analysis but also imply the hard core of the microeconomics research programme, the reader need only peruse the contents of any (orthodox) microeconomics textbook. Such a perusal will quickly reveal that numerous theories embodying the instructions laid down in the positive heuristic of the microeconomics research programme have been constructed in an attempt to provide explanations and predictions for a very wide range of phenomena.

As we have just noted, the positive heuristic of a research programme will lead to a series of theories T_1, T_2, T_3, . . . being produced within the programme. This immediately raises the important question: how do we appraise this temporal sequence of theories? In other words, how do we appraise the development of a research programme over time? As we shall see below, the answer provided by MSRP is designed to enable us to appraise the development of a research programme as either *progressive* or *degenerating*. Thus, in the following two sub-sections, we shall present the rules of appraisal which MSRP uses in order to give a research programme either a *positive* appraisal or a *negative* appraisal *at a particular point in time*.

A progressive research programme

According to MSRP, a research programme is appraised as *progressive* (at a particular point in time) if the series of theories which it produces fulfil the following conditions:

1. Each new theory in the series is capable of explaining the previous successes of the preceding theory in the series. In other words, all the unrefuted testable consequences or predictions contained in the preceding theory T_{n-1} are also contained in its successor T_n.
2. Each new theory in the series contains refutable consequences or predictions that are additional (and novel) to those contained in the preceding theory in the series. In other words, theory T_n has more testable consequences than its predecessor T_{n-1}.
3. Some of the additional (novel) testable consequences or predictions of theory T_n have been confirmed by reproducible empirical tests.

Note that the above appraisal of a research programme as progressive involves a *theoretical* aspect of appraisal complemented by an *empirical* aspect of appraisal. The first two conditions contain the theoretical aspect of appraisal and, consequently, a series of theories is appraised as *theoretically progressive* if these two conditions are fulfilled. The third condition contains the empirical aspect of appraisal and, consequently, a series of theoretically progressive theories is appraised as being also *empirically progressive* if this condition is fulfilled. Hence a series of theories is appraised as progressive if it is *both* theoretically and empirically progressive.

A degenerating research programme

On the other hand, a research programme is appraised as *degenerating* (at a particular point in time) if the series of theories produced within it is not *both* theoretically and empirically progressive. In this degenerating phase of a research programme *theoretical degeneracy* occurs as the programme persistently fails to produce additional novel refutable predictions. Instead of producing protective belt modifications which both increase the range of refutable predictions and increasingly accommodate existing anomalies, the modifications in this theoretically degenerate phase are increasingly *ad hoc* in character and, therefore, only serve to reduce (or fail to increase) the range of refutable predictions. Moreover, if the predictions provided by these *ad hoc* modifications of the protective belt also fail to be empirically confirmed then *empirical degeneracy* also occurs.

It is important to note that a research programme is also appraised as degenerating if it manifests theoretical progression along with empirical degeneracy. Thus, if theory T_n contains refutable predictions that are additional to those contained in its predecessor T_{n-1}, but none of these additional predictions succeed in getting empirically confirmed, then not only are the modifications of the protective belt that produced these additional predictions classed as *ad hoc* but also the research programme is appraised as degenerating. In other words, if the series of theories produced within a research programme is not *both* theoretically and empirically progressive it is appraised as degenerating.

It is also important to note that MSRP appraises a research programme as degenerating in the case where the programme does produce additional new refutable predictions, but where these additional predictions are the outcome of a patched, makeshift, arbitrary series of disconnected theories rather than the outcome of a coherent series of theories produced under the guidance of the research programme's positive heuristic.

To appreciate this point note that if a research programme faces logical and empirical difficulties, we would expect the economics researchers involved to try to overcome these difficulties by modifying the programme's protective belt in accordance with its positive heuristic. Since these modifications are guided by the positive heuristic, then they will involve phenomena that can be explained within the scope of the programme's theories. This, in turn, means that the empirical confirmation of the predictions flowing from these modifications will have precise meaning in the sense that it can be readily related to the explanation provided by the programme's theories.

In contrast, if these modifications are arbitrary and unrelated to the programme's positive heuristic, then they will likely involve phenomena which cannot be adequately explained within the scope of the programme's theories. Hence, even if these modifications lead to predictions which are empirically confirmed, this empirical evidence is ambiguous in the sense that it relates to phenomena which cannot be adequately explained within the scope of the programme's theories. Consequently, not only does MSRP class the latter modifications as *ad hoc* but it also appraises the research programme as degenerating.

(Note that the above discussion has introduced three types of *ad hoc* modifications of the protective belt. Thus we have (1) modifications which either reduce or fail to increase the range of refutable predictions (known as *ad* hoc_1), and (2) modifications which have increased the range of refutable predictions but none of these additional predictions have succeeded in getting empirically confirmed (known as *ad* hoc_2), and (3) modifications which may both increase the range of refutable predictions and be empirically confirmed, but which are not in accordance with the research programme's positive heuristic (known as *ad* hoc_3). Also, note that this classification implies that non-*ad hoc* modifications of the protective belt are those which increase the range of refutable predictions in accordance with the research programme's positive heuristic and which also are empirically confirmed. In other words, non-*ad hoc* modifications are those which are in accordance with the research programme's positive heuristic and which result in *both* theoretical and empirical progression.)

Now that we have provided an introductory account of both the historical development of a research programme and its methodological appraisal, we shall proceed to a somewhat more detailed examination of this account.

6.2 THE MINOR ROLE OF EMPIRICAL REFUTATIONS UNDER MSRP

The first important point we wish to highlight, particularly in contrast to falsificationism, is that empirical refutations of existing theories are no longer regarded as the crucial driving force leading to the proposal of new theories and hence to the growth of economic knowledge. Rather, in the MSRP account, the positive heuristic of a research programme is regarded as the major driving force leading to the proposal of new theories and hence to the growth of economic knowledge. Moreover, not only is the positive heuristic regarded as the major driving force underlying a research programme but it is also regarded as being capable of generating a succession of theories *quite independently of any empirical refutations.*

Since the positive heuristic of a research programme contains a roughly specified plan both for developing existing theories and for generating new rival theories, this means that the positive heuristic will generate a fairly constant proliferation of theories quite independently of any empirical refutations. In addition to this, since the positive heuristic may also contain guidelines as to how to resolve logical difficulties or inconsistencies (that arise in the development of the research programme) via certain non-*ad hoc* modifications of the protective belt hypotheses, this will further stimulate the proliferation of theories.

Thus, the greater the *heuristic power* of a research programme (that is, the more detailed and extensive the guidelines contained in its positive heuristic) the greater will be the programme's potentiality for generating a succession of new theories in accordance with its positive heuristic. Also, the greater the heuristic power of a research programme, the greater will be the positive heuristic's ability both to point to shortcomings in existing theories and to lay down guidelines for their replacement quite independently of any empirical refutations.

According to MSRP, it is not empirical refutations of existing theories, but rather the positive heuristic of a research programme which mainly determines the choice of problems that economics researchers work on, and which serves as the major stimulus to the proliferation of theories. (For example, as noted in Section 6.1 above, the positive heuristic of the foregoing microeconomics research programme, which was introduced in Chapter 5, not only guides economics researchers to work on optimization problems and equilibrium problems but also stimulates the production of theories using these analytical techniques).

While this is so, it should be noted that MSRP does not exclude the possibility that the empirical refutation of existing theories may also act as an important stimulus to the modification of these theories and/or to the proposal of new theories. However, the important point in MSRP is that the positive heuristic is regarded as playing a *major* role in stimulating theory proliferation. In contrast, empirical refutations are regarded as playing only a *minor* role in stimulating theory proliferation.

The falsification of a theory under MSRP

In addition to noting that empirical refutations play a smaller role under MSRP than under falsificationism, it is important to note also that under MSRP the falsification of a theory, within the series of theories produced by a research programme, differs from the falsification of a theory under falsificationism. Under the latter, the falsification of theory T_{n-1} is essentially the outcome of a two-cornered fight between that theory and empirical tests. While researchers may have proposed a rival theory T_n prior to the empirical falsification of T_{n-1}, the emergence of T_n is not a necessary aspect of the falsification of T_{n-1}. The falsification of T_{n-1} is solely the outcome of the two-cornered fight between T_{n-1} and empirical tests.

In contrast, according to MSRP, theory T_{n-1} is not regarded as falsified *until* a better theory T_n emerges. Thus, for example, if certain consequences or predictions of T_{n-1} are refuted by reproducible empirical tests, this does not mean that T_{n-1} is then automatically regarded as falsified. Rather, T_{n-1} is only regarded as falsified when a better theory emerges. Hence, for T_n to qualify as a better theory, and for T_{n-1} to be therefore regarded as falsified, T_n must (a) contain all the unrefuted predictions that are contained in T_{n-1}, and

(b) contain additional novel predictions not contained in T_{n-1} (with these novel predictions being improbable in the light of, or even forbidden by, T_{n-1}), and (c) have some of these novel predictions empirically confirmed.

It is essential to note that, under MSRP, T_{n-1} can be regarded as refuted even though it has so far successfully passed all empirical tests. If T_n satisfies the 'progressive' conditions, noted under (a), (b), and (c) in the preceding paragraph, then the emergence of T_n is also taken as the 'refutation' of T_{n-1}. In other words, empirical refutations are not necessary for the falsification of T_{n-1}. Rather, falsification of T_{n-1} may take place when it is superseded by a better or more 'progressive' theory T_n *quite independently of empirical refutations.*

It is also essential to note that the appraisal of T_n as a better theory than T_{n-1} still holds even though both T_{n-1} and T_n may have been born refuted. Moreover, under MSRP, T_n may still be appraised as a better theory than T_{n-1} not only in the case where both T_{n-1} and T_n have been born refuted, but also in the case where both T_{n-1} and T_n have equally failed to pass certain other empirical tests. Provided T_n satisfies the previously noted 'progressive' conditions, then it is regarded as a better theory than T_{n-1} despite the fact that both theories may face a variety of common empirical refutations. In other words, *under MSRP various prediction failures can be tolerated within a research programme as long as some theoretical and empirical progress is being made.*

(Note that MSRP, in common with various other methodological procedures, faces a commensurability problem in the case where the comparison of T_n and T_{n-1} involves both a loss as well as a gain in empirically-confirmed explanatory content. While advocates of MSRP are well aware that there are difficulties in comparing the content of theories in such cases, they argue that objective comparison can nonetheless still be made. For a suggested solution to the content-comparison problem, see Watkins [1984], Chapter 5.)

The foregoing discussion indicates that, under MSRP, empirical refutations have a much less important role in the growth of economic knowledge than is envisaged under falsificationism. Also, it indicates that falsification is no longer viewed as involving just a theory and empirical observations. Rather, it is now viewed as involving competing theories as well as empirical observations. Under MSRP the crucial element in falsification is whether a new theory T_n contains additional novel predictions, that are not contained in its predecessor T_{n-1}, and whether some of these novel predictions are empirically confirmed. In other words, MSRP transfers the emphasis away from empirical refutations and focuses it instead on *empirical confirmations of the additional novel predictions contained in the new theory*.

Note, however, that the emphasis is not simply on *any* empirical confirmations of a theory, but rather on the empirical confirmations of the *additional novel* predictions contained in that theory. Consequently, progression within a research programme is viewed as being marked by empirical tests confirming the additional novel predictions of new theories rather than by empirical tests falsifying the predictions of existing theories. Since such confirmations are taken as an indication that a new theory is better than its predecessor then, under MSRP, the growth of economic knowledge will be characterized by each theory (in the series of theories produced by a research programme) being falsified, in turn, when it is superseded by a better or more progressive theory.

Heuristic power and appraisal

Finally, before proceeding further in our discussion of MSRP, let us once more underline (as we have already done both in our discussion of the appraisal of the historical development of a research programme and in our discussion of the minor role of empirial refutations under MSRP) the vital role played by the positive heuristic of a research programme in the growth of economic knowledge.

As we have seen, the greater the heuristic power of a research programme the more detailed and extensive will be its positive heuristic, and hence the greater the programme's potentiality for generating a succession of new theories containing additional testable consequences or predictions. Also, the greater the heuristic power of a research programme the greater its potentiality for accommodating various empirical refutations that have been encountered in the development of the research programme. Consequently, under MSRP, a research programme can also be appraised (at a particular point in time) for its degree of *heuristic power*. Hence a research programme will be given a *positive* appraisal if it possesses strong heuristic power in addition to containing a theoretically and empirically progressive series of theories. Contrariwise, a research programme will be given a *negative* appraisal if it possesses a positive heuristic which is weak or exhausted in addition to containing a theoretically and empirically degenerating series of theories.

6.3 THE HIGH DEGREE OF AUTONOMY OF THEORETICAL ECONOMICS

In the foregoing sections, we noted the importance of a research programme's heuristic power. Having done so, we are now in a position to see how MSRP can explain why economics research may often be characterized by numerous theoretical developments which are accompanied by both a relatively small amount of empirical testing and a relatively small concern about empirical refutations.

To do this, let us first recall that the positive heuristic of a research programme serves as the driving force responsible for generating a series of new theories. Also, recall that if each new theory in this series contains testable predictions that are additional to those contained in its predecessor, then theoretical progression takes place. Finally, recall that if some of these additional testable predictions are subsequently confirmed by empirical tests then, according to MSRP, the research programme has progressed (since progression within a research programme requires *both* theoretical and empirical progression).

Note, however, that while theoretical progression can be checked relatively quickly (via logical analysis, which can readily determine whether or not a new theory does indeed contain additional testable predictions), empirical progression can only be checked by empirical testing which (for example, if suitable data are not readily available) may take a considerable time.

Consequently, while the positive heuristic continues to generate new theories, and while the empirical testing of these new theories lags considerably behind their generation, economics research will inevitably be characterized by numerous theoretical developments which are largely unaccompanied by empirical testing. In other words, during such periods, theoretical economics will experience a *high degree of autonomy* in the sense that the positive heuristic is generating theoretical developments almost completely independently of empirical testing (and hence almost completely independently of either empirical confirmations or empirical refutations).

Moreover, according to MSRP, during such periods the main research difficulties are analytical (and hence usually mathematical) ones rather than ones arising from empirical refutations. The explanation given for this is that, during such periods, the main emphasis is on theoretical development in accordance with the research programme's positive heuristic which, in turn, will usually imply both the use and development of mathematical techniques appropriate to this theoretical development.

It is important to note that, while MSRP can explain why certain periods of research in economics may be characterized by a high degree of autonomy of theoretical economics, the existence of such theoretical autonomy in economics complicates the whole question of appraising research programmes. The ways in which it does so will be considered in detail in Chapter 7.

The positive heuristic and simultaneous research discoveries

Not only does the heuristic power of a research programme enable us to explain the high degree of autonomy of theoretical economics, but it also helps to explain why theoretical breakthroughs in economics often come in bursts of very similar theories. Since the various aspects of a research programme are public property (in the sense that not only the problems being considered within the research programme, but also the research programme's positive heuristic for resolving these problems, are publicly discussed in widely-accessible economics journals), then it is not surprising that researchers working independently of one another (perhaps in different parts of the world), but working within the same research programme, produce almost identical solutions to their common problems.

In other words, the positive heuristic of a research programme helps us to understand why the historical development of that programme is often characterized by bursts of simultaneous theoretical innovations (see Urbach [1978]). Also, it helps us to understand why a particular theoretical breakthrough, in a given research programme, may be quickly followed by a burst of further, very similar, theoretical developments (which are the outcome of many researchers, within the same research programme and hence with the same positive heuristic, simultaneously attempting both to apply and to develop that particular theoretical breakthrough).

The positive heuristic and theory-conception

Recall that, in Chapters 2 and 4, we noted that while economists are clearly capable of conceiving or inventing theories or hypotheses it is by no means clear how they do so. Recall also, with regard to this difficulty, that we simply assumed that economists are capable of conceiving theories and, therefore, deliberately left the analysis of the mental processes by which they do so to those who wish to investigate the complex realm of the psychology of knowledge. Consequently, throughout our discussion in Chapters 2 and 4, we assumed not only that economists were somehow capable of conceiving theories, but also that in some rather unclear and undefined way these theoretical conceptions were influenced by both a previous knowledge of the subject under study and an appreciation of the problems related to the study of this subject.

However, now that we have encountered MSRP's account of the role of a research programme's positive heuristic, we have additional insight into the process of theory-conception within a research programme. In other words, most theories do not just spring suddenly into existence as the outcome of a completely unguided flash of inspiration, rather they are the outcome of (still somewhat mysterious) inspiration aided by the guidelines or suggestions contained in the research programme's positive heuristic (see Urbach [1978]).

6.4 MSRP AND THE DUHEM PROBLEM

Now that we have fuller knowledge of the component parts of Lakatosian research programmes, we can proceed not only to outline MSRP's solution of the Duhem problem but also to provide a rationale for the methodological decision which renders the hard core of a research programme irrefutable.

In our earlier discussion of falsificationism, we noted that the Duhem problem arises when a theory or hypothesis appears to be falsified by empirical tests. Since, in such a situation, we are always testing a particular hypothesis together with numerous other hypotheses, then we are faced with the Duhem problem of not knowing which of the hypotheses is responsible for the apparent falsification. Moreover, since we do not know which hypothesis should be regarded as falsified, then we do not know which one should be replaced or modified.

The falsificationist's solution to the Duhem problem

As noted in Chapter 4, the falsificationist's solution to the Duhem problem essentially involves letting the particular hypothesis in question bear the brunt of the empirical tests. In other words, it is regarded as responsible for the empirical refutation and is therefore regarded as falsified. This, in turn, means that the falsificationist's attention is mainly directed towards either the replacement or modification of this particular hypothesis. The falsificationist is well aware that this solution is risky (since a hypothesis may be erroneously regarded as falsified when the source of the falsification is actually located elsewhere), but he feels that this solution will not only encourage a critical (rather than a defensive) attitude but will also encourage the growth of economic knowledge.

Thus, under falsificationism, the theory or hypothesis in question is made to bear the brunt of empirical refutation and is therefore declared falsified. This, in turn, is assumed to lead either to the proposal of new theories or to the non-*ad hoc* modification of existing theories and hence to the growth of economic knowledge.

The MSRP solution to the Duhem problem

The MSRP solution to the Duhem problem is rather different from that of falsificationism. One immediate difference is that MSRP permits an apparent empirical refutation to be simply noted as an anomaly and shelved for future consideration. Thus the positive heuristic of a research programme may suggest that it is best to proceed with the research programme, ignoring the anomaly for the present time, in the hope that it can be accommodated (by some non-*ad hoc* modification of the protective belt) at a later stage in the development of the programme.

Moreover, MSRP does not require that the particular hypothesis or theory facing apparent falsification should necessarily be replaced or modified. Rather MSRP permits researchers to replace or modify *any* (non-hard-core) hypothesis or theory within the research programme in question, and appraises the best modification to be that which generates most (theoretical and empirical) progression over the preceding situation. Consequently, under MSRP, it is only when a hypothesis or theory is progressively replaced by another hypothesis or theory that it is regarded as falsified.

It is important to note that not only does MSRP permit any progressive modification, but it also provides us with useful insight as to *how* this modification takes place. Thus, as noted earlier, the greater the heuristic power of a research programme the greater will be the positive heuristic's ability not only to point to shortcomings in existing theories (even independently of empirical refutations), but also to lay down guidelines for their replacement or modification.

A rationale for not modifying hard core hypotheses

It is important also to note that MSRP is well aware that researchers may wish to respond to empirical refutations by modifying the *hard core hypotheses* of a research programme. However, as MSRP points out, there is much to discourage researchers from taking such a course of action.

To appreciate why this is so, recall that a research programme is composed of the hard core hypotheses plus the protective belt hypotheses. Also, recall that the positive heuristic of a research programme provides a set of suggestions as to how the hard core hypotheses of the programme are to be supplemented, both by the generation and the modification of protective belt hypotheses, in order for the programme to be capable of providing explanations and predictions of the phenomena under consideration. Finally, in recalling these features of a research programme, note that a research programme is very much an organized structure of linked hypotheses. In other words, a research programme consists of groupings of hypotheses viewed as a *structural whole*, with the hard core hypotheses and the protective belt hypotheses being closely linked in the sense that the protective belt hypotheses are essentially envisaged as being 'built around' the hard core hypotheses in accordance with the positive heuristic of the programme.

Consequently, because of this unified structure, the attempt to modify the hard core of a research programme will essentially involve abandoning the whole programme. This is so because the move to a new hard core will mean that a new protective belt will have to be constructed which, in turn, will likely mean that a new positive heuristic (and hence certain new analytical techniques) will also have to be constructed.

When one considers that the move to a new hard core essentially means that a whole new programme will have to be built up (unless there is an existing alternative research programme to which researchers can switch), then it is clear that there is much to discourage researchers from undertaking such a massive task. To abandon the hard core of a research programme is essentially to abandon the whole programme and start all over again in a theoretical void!

By way of contrast, if researchers hold on to the existing hard core, and to the existing programme, and hence to its existing positive heuristic, then this positive heuristic will guide their attempts to modify the programme's protective belt. In other words, the benefit of staying with the current programme is that it provides guidance for the future development of the research programme. Consequently, in situations where the advantages of sticking with the existing hard core of a research programme exceed the disadvantages of modifying that hard core, we have a rationale for the methodological decision that the hard core is to remain unmodified and intact during the development of the programme (see Worrall [1978b]). This, in turn, implies that we also have a rationale for the methodological decision that modifications are to take place in the protective belt.

6.5 THE COMPARISON OF RESEARCH PROGRAMMES

So far, in our discussion, we have only been concerned with appraising the explanatory power of a particular research programme. However, in practice, it is likely that there are one or more competing research programmes which also claim to explain the phenomena under consideration. This, in turn, means that MSRP is faced with the problem of comparing rival research programmes. Hence, in this section, we shall now proceed to an examination of MSRP's proposals for handling this problem. In doing so, note that we shall deliberately refrain from giving examples of research programmes which, for example, may compete with the foregoing microeconomics research programme (introduced in Chapter 5). In other words, at this stage, we shall merely concentrate on providing a general account of the MSRP proposals for comparing rival research programmes. In Chapter 8, when we return to this area of discussion in more detail, we shall provide examples of competing research programmes.

Criteria for evaluating rival research programmes

According to MSRP, the relative merits of competing research programmes are to be evaluated by reference to their respective degrees of explanatory power. If one research programme explains more than a competing research programme, then it is regarded as being superior to its competitor. In other words, in such comparisons, if one research programme is capable not only of explaining the previous successes of a rival research programme but also of providing additional novel explanatory content which has been empirically confirmed then, according to MSRP, it is regarded as being superior to its rival.

Moreover, according to MSRP, the superiority of one research programme in relation to another is not only to be judged (as in the preceding paragraph) by determining which research programme is the most progressive. Rather the evaluation of the relative merits of research programmes also includes a comparison of each research programme's heuristic strength. Consequently, a more progressive, heuristically stronger research programme is regarded as superior to a less progressive, heuristically weaker research programme.

The comparison of rival research programmes can be problematic

It is important to note, however, that the comparison of research programmes is not so straightforward as it may first appear. For example, one problem in this respect arises from the possibility that a research programme, which has continually degenerated for some period of time, may stage a comeback and, reversing its past performance, subsequently succeed in being continually progressive for a long period of time. This recognition that a degenerating research programme may still stage a comeback (via some ingenious modification of its protective belt that results in both theoretical and empirical progress) means that we cannot conclusively appraise one research programme as superior to another for all time. In other words, while *at any given point in time* we can, via MSRP, evaluate one research programme as superior to another, we must recognize that this evaluation may be reversed in the future.

While it is important to note the foregoing problem, it is also important to note that it would be extremely unrealistic to expect MSRP (or any other method of appraisal) to be able to provide a means whereby we could appraise the *future* performance of a research programme. This is especially so when we remember the obvious unpredictability of the outcome of research activity.

However, before leaving this point, it should be noted that MSRP enables us to make a particular type of assessment of the potential for future development of a research programme. Thus, according to MSRP, it is claimed that a research programme with a powerful heuristic is likely to produce greater theoretical progress than a heuristically weaker rival. In other words, while there is no guarantee that heuristic strength will guarantee future progression in the sense of *both* theoretical and empirical progress, it is claimed that future theoretical progress is more likely to be associated with higher heuristic strength. Hence, in this inevitably restricted sense (since there is no guarantee of the future empirical success of any research programme), MSRP enables us to make some prediction of the potential for future development of a research programme (see Urbach [1978]).

A further problem, associated with the comparison of rival research programmes, arises in the situation where a long-established, extensive, degenerating research programme is being compared with a recently-introduced, progressive research programme. In such a situation, the degenerating older research programme may still be regarded as superior to the younger progressive research programme in the sense that the latter has not yet generated greater (empirically-confirmed) explanatory content than the former. Moreover, it may take a considerable period of time before the new programme is capable of generating this excess explanatory content. Consequently, in such situations, MSRP stresses the importance of methodological tolerance and urges that the development of young progressive research programmes should be encouraged.

Yet another problem, associated with comparing one research programme (denoted as RP_2) with its rival (denoted as RP_1), arises in the situation where (1) RP_2 contains some, but not all, of the empirically-confirmed explanatory content of RP_1, and (2) RP_2

contains an additional amount of empirically-confirmed explanatory content not contained in RP_1. In other words, how do we compare research programmes in situations where a loss as well as a gain in explanatory content is involved?

In earlier chapters, we noted that philosophers have suggested ways of solving such content-comparison problems (for example, see Watkins [1984], Chapter 5). However, it is interesting to note that even if this content-comparison problem *remains unresolved* (perhaps due to practical difficulties in implementing suggested solutions to this problem), MSRP can still provide grounds for preferring one programme to another. If, for example, RP_2 is both more progressive and heuristically stronger than RP_1, then the advocates of MSRP argue that RP_2 is more likely than RP_1 to make good the explanatory losses incurred in adopting it (see Worrall [1978a], p. 63). This ability, to discriminate between RP_2 and RP_1 in such situations, is viewed by advocates of MSRP as a considerable improvement on falsificationism.

Essentially the advocates of MSRP consider that the long-run growth of economic knowledge will be furthered most by a succession of progressive research programmes. Thus, while the truth of any particular theory (produced within any of these research programmes and hence occupying a position within the temporal sequence of theories produced by the succession of progressive research programmes) is not certain, and while the convergence of this series of theories towards the truth is not certain either, it is conjectured that the succession of progressive research programmes is likely to produce theories which are ever-closer approximations to the truth.

(Note that Lakatos, in common with Popper, has not only taken increasing versimilitude as the aim of science but he has also been criticized for failing to establish that MSRP provides the methodological means to this end. Just as Popper's link between corroboration and versimilitude has been criticized, so also Lakatos's link between the corroboration of the novel predictions of a research programme and versimilitude has been criticized (for example, see Newton-Smith [1981], Chapter 4). For a suggested way round this criticism, see Newton-Smith [1981], Chapters 8 and 9.)

Finally, before leaving this section, it should be noted that further aspects of this complex problem of comparing research programmes will be discussed in Chapter 8.

6.6 SUMMARY OF THE WAYS IN WHICH MSRP IMPROVES ON FALSIFICATIONISM

At this point, we shall briefly summarize the claimed advantages of MSRP over falsificationism. Subsequently, in Chapters 7 and 8, we shall examine in more detail the implications of adopting MSRP in economics.

As noted in the preceding chapter, the falsificationist account essentially concentrates on the relationship between *individual* theories or hypotheses and empirical observations. However, an examination of actual practice indicates that economists are always considering a temporal sequence of *groupings* of hypotheses rather than a temporal sequence of individual hypotheses. This, in turn, means that we require a methodology that not only explicitly deals with groupings of hypotheses but also attempts to explain why one grouping of hypotheses is preferred to another. Hence, since MSRP does just this, it is claimed to be an improvement on falsificationism.

In addition to being specifically concerned with groupings of hypotheses, MSRP also explicitly recognizes that researchers are generally involved in a fairly definite research *programme*. This, in turn, means that the group of hypotheses constituting a research programme is not only viewed as a structural whole but also it is viewed as possessing a temporal continuity. Consequently, MSRP is claimed to provide a significant improvement on falsificationism by both recognizing this programmatic aspect and incorporating it into methodological appraisal.

MSRP further claims to have remedied another deficiency of falsificationism by both introducing the *heuristic* aspect of economics research and incorporating it into methodological appraisals. Thus, as we have already seen, MSRP introduces the negative and positive heuristics of a research programme which provide, respectively, guidance about what paths of research to avoid and what paths of research to pursue. Also, as noted earlier, MSRP puts considerable emphasis on the heuristic strength of a research programme, even to the extent of explicitly including assessment of heuristic strength when appraising a research programme.

This emphasis, in turn, arises from the fact that MSRP sees the positive heuristic of a research programme as the major driving force underlying both the development of a research programme and, by implication (when applied to the case of economics), the growth of economic knowledge. Consequently, the introduction of the heuristic aspect can be claimed as an important improvement over falsificationism in the sense that it provides additional useful insights not only into various aspects of economics research but also into the growth of economic knowledge.

For example, as we have already seen, the positive heuristic of a research programme gives considerable insight into what mainly determines the choice of problems that economics researchers work on within a given research programme, as well as providing insight into what guides the development and modification of existing theories within the programme. Also, the positive heuristic gives important insight not only into what guides the production of new theories within a research programme (plus a limited insight into the process of theory-conception), but also into what guides researchers' responses to logical and empirical difficulties that arise in the development of the programme.

In addition to these insights, the positive heuristic also helps to explain why some periods are characterized by theoretical developments that are accompanied by both a relatively small amount of empirical testing and a relatively low concern about either empirical confirmations or empirical refutations. Moreover, the positive heuristic also helps to explain why theoretical breakthroughs in economics often come in bursts of very similar theories. Lastly, it also enables us to make some prediction of the potential for future development of a research programme.

A further claimed advantage of MSRP over falsificationism relates to the criticism that falsificationism is inadequate on historical grounds. Thus, as we saw at the beginning of Chapter 5, falsificationism is unable to explain adequately not only why certain falsifying evidence is often ignored by economics researchers, but also why one theory may be regarded as superior to its predecessor even though both theories were born refuted. Since MSRP attempts to provide a rationale for both these situations, it is claimed to be an improvement over falsificationism. Hence, while it is irrational under falsificationism to ignore the empirical refutations in both these situations, it is rational under MSRP for researchers to follow the advice of the research programme's positive heuristic to ignore temporarily these refutations (in the hope that they will be later accommodated by some non-*ad hoc* modification of the programme's protective belt).

Also, while falsificationism gives us no grounds for preferring theory T_2 over theory T_1 when both theories have been born refuted, MSRP enables us to appraise T_2 as a better theory than T_1 provided T_2 is more progressive than T_1. In other words, in contrast to falsificationism, MSRP permits various empirical refutations to be tolerated within a research programme as long as some theoretical and empirical progress is being made.

MSRP also claims to have improved on falsificationism by providing a better explanation of the role of competing theories in the process of falsification. Thus, whereas under falsificationism the falsification of a theory is restricted essentially to the outcome of a two-cornered fight between that theory and empirical observations, under MSRP a theory is not regarded as falsified until a better theory comes along. In other words, MSRP views falsification as necessarily involving competing theories as well as empirical observations.

Moreover, in the process of falsification under MSRP, the emphasis is transferred away from empirical refutations and instead is focussed on empirical confirmations of the additional novel predictions contained in the competing theory or theories. It is claimed that this change of emphasis accords better with studies of the actual practice of researchers. Finally, with regard to the de-emphasis on empirical refutations, MSRP also claims that the positive heuristic of a research programme provides a better explanation of the driving force leading to the generation of new theories (and hence to the growth of scientific knowledge) than does empirical refutation under falsificationism.

With regard to the commensurability problem, MSRP claims to have improved on falsificationism by being able to provide certain guidance in such situations.

Lastly, with regard to the Duhem problem, MSRP claims to have improved on falsificationism by providing a solution to this problem which is not only less risky but which also accords better with studies of the actual practice of researchers. Thus, as we have seen, rather than let the particular theory or hypothesis in question bear the brunt of apparent refutations, MSRP permits researchers to replace or modify any (non-hard-core) theory or hypothesis within the research programme concerned. Moreover, it is also claimed that the positive heuristic of a research programme provides important insight into how researchers respond to the Duhem problem (in the sense that it guides the modification of the research programme's protective belt).

References for further reading

In addition to the references given to Lakatos at the end of Chapter 5, further development of MSRP can be found in Urbach [1978]; Worrall [1978a] and [1978b]; and Zahar [1978].

Expositions of MSRP can also be found in Blaug [1980a], pp. 34-40; Caldwell [1982], pp. 85-9; Chalmers [1982], Chapter 7; Koertge [1979b]; Losee [1980], pp. 208-12; Newton-Smith [1981], Chapter 4; and Suppe [1977], pp. 659-70.

7 Implications of Adopting MSRP in Economics—I

In this chapter we shall extend our discussion of MSRP to include an examination of some of the implications of adopting MSRP in economics. In doing so, we shall initially restrict our discussion to the case of a *given* research programme. Then, in Chapter 8, we shall remove this restriction in order to also include *competing* research programmes in the discussion.

7.1 MSRP AND APPRAISAL WITHIN A RESEARCH PROGRAMME

Let us suppose that economics researchers have decided to adopt MSRP as their method of appraisal. Given this situation, we can then note that while the adoption of MSRP will not provide these researchers with precise guidance as to how to solve the various research problems they face, the adoption of MSRP will suggest certain ways of both *approaching* and *appraising* their research activity.

Thus if economics researchers have adopted MSRP as suitable to their research situation, then we would also expect them to recognize that their research activity is part of a research *programme*. This, in turn, means that we would expect them to view this research programme as an organized structure of linked groupings of hypotheses. Consequently, in this situation, we would expect them also to be able to identify which group of hypotheses constitutes the *hard core* of the research programme and which group of hypotheses constitutes the *protective belt* of the research programme.

In addition, once economics researchers have adopted MSRP,

we would expect them to follow the *negative heuristic* advice that the hard core of the research programme is not to be rejected or modified during the development of the programme. Also, we would expect them to be able to identify (and follow the advice of) the *positive heuristic* of the research programme, not only with its research agenda and its guidance about how to develop and modify the protective belt hypotheses, but also with its guidance about how to cope with logical and empirical difficulties which arise in the development of the programme.

As the research activity proceeds, the positive heuristic of the research programme will lead to a series of theories or hypotheses being produced within the programme. Given that economics researchers have adopted the MSRP method of appraisal, then this temporal sequence of theories (containing not only a succession of new theories but also the auxiliary hypotheses that accompany each of these new theories) will be appraised as progressive or degenerating depending upon whether or not it is both theoretically and empirically progressive.

In other words, MSRP directs researchers to consider both whether each successive new theory in the series contains additional novel testable predictions and whether some of these additional predictions have been empirically confirmed. Moreover, not only does MSRP guide researchers to appraise groupings of theories in this way, but it also makes competing theories an essential part of this appraisal procedure. Hence, as we saw in the previous chapter, a theory is only regarded as falsified when it is superseded by a rival theory which is more progressive. Also, when researchers are assessing the merits of competing theories, MSRP directs them to prefer the theory which is the most progressive.

While the above discussion indicates how the adoption of MSRP will provide economics researchers with suggestions for both approaching and appraising their research activity, it is important to note that the adoption of MSRP may not be quite so straightforward as it appears. For example, as we shall see below, certain difficulties arise in relation to the hard core/protective belt distinction and also in relation to situations of theoretical autonomy.

7.2 THE HARD CORE/PROTECTIVE BELT DISTINCTION

As noted above, if economics researchers have adopted MSRP as their method of appraisal, we would then expect them to be able to draw a clear distinction between hard core hypotheses and protective belt hypotheses. But this immediately raises the question of how the researchers are actually going to arrive at this clear distinction in practice. How, for example, will they be able to identify which hypotheses are to be classed as hard core hypotheses and therefore regarded as irrefutable? Does MSRP provide definite guidance as to how the hard core hypotheses are to be identified? The answer, unfortunately, is that MSRP does not provide such guidance. MSRP simply states that hard core hypotheses are rendered unfalsifiable by the methodological decision of the participants in the given research programme, it does not give any guidance either as to how these hypotheses are to be identified or as to how this methodological decision is to be arrived at.

Clearly, MSRP's lack of guidance as to how researchers are to arrive at a clear-cut hard core/protective belt distinction raises serious problems. What, for example, happens in the (not unlikely) situation where individual researchers may not only have different views about what assumptions or hypotheses should be classed as basic and fundamental to the research programme, but also may change their views over the period that they are working in the research programme? Obviously, if researchers' views about what hypotheses constitute the hard core are neither sufficiently uniform nor sufficiently constant over time, then it will not be possible to arrive at a clear distinction between hard core and protective belt hypotheses.

While MSRP does not provide any insight into the actual process by which the hard core/protective belt distinction is to be made, it does however assume that such a distinction will eventually emerge within each research programme. Thus, according to MSRP, while the early stages of development of a research programme will be characterized by considerable experimentation and difference of opinion as to which hypotheses should be regarded as fundamental to the programme, the later, mature stage of development of a research programme will contain a widely-accepted, unchanging hard core. In other words, MSRP assumes that the hard core of a research programme will eventually emerge via a long process of trial and error.

Hence, MSRP argues, if we confine our attention to mature research programmes, then a clear-cut hard core/protective belt distinction can be readily made, since the historical maturing of each research programme will have made clear exactly which hypotheses are fundamental to that research programme (in the sense that these hypotheses eventually emerged as those which the programme has consistently held on to in the face of logical and empirical difficulties). In other words, if we confine our attention to the cases of well-articulated, mature research programmes, then we will be dealing with cases where the methodological decision to render certain hypotheses unfalsifiable has already been taken.

A modified form of MSRP

If we accept the MSRP argument that well-articulated, mature research programmes will have a clearly recognizable hard core, and hence a clearly recognizable protective belt, then the MSRP method of appraisal can be applied to such programmes. But what about budding, immature research programmes? Is the MSRP method of appraisal of no relevance to such programmes? One response to this question is that a modified form of MSRP can be applied in such cases.

In order to appreciate this modified form of MSRP, let us first note that an alternative way of identifying a research programme has been suggested by Cross (1982a). Thus, Cross has suggested that instead of identifying linked groupings of hypotheses as a distinct research programme, because these groupings of hypotheses contain both a clearly identifiable hard core/protective belt distinction and a distinctive positive heuristic, such linked groupings of hypotheses could alternatively be identified as a distinct research programme by their distinctive positive heuristic alone. Therefore once a research programme has been identified solely by its distinctive positive heuristic, then the series of theories or hypotheses which it produces can be appraised as either progressive or degenerating using the method of appraisal suggested by MSRP. Consequently, it can be argued that MSRP, in this modified form, can still be applied to situations where the hard core/protective belt distinction is not clear-cut.

Do we need the hard core/protective belt distinction?

The argument of the preceding paragraph, suggesting that research programmes can be identified solely by their distinctive positive heuristic and then appraised via the MSRP appraisal criteria, immediately raises the question of whether we need the hard core/ protective belt distinction at all. If we can proceed to appraise research programmes despite having abandoned this distinction, and hence having abandoned the negative heuristic aspect of a research programme, then is there any good reason why we should not abandon the hard core/protective belt distinction altogether when appraising research programmes in economics? It is our opinion that there *is* good reason for retaining this distinction and, consequently, we shall examine this point in more detail in Chapter 8. For the moment, however, let us simply note that MSRP can be used in situations where the hard core/protective belt distinction is clearly recognizable and, if necessary, a modified form of MSRP can be used in situations where this distinction is not clear-cut.

7.3 MSRP AND THEORETICAL AUTONOMY

As we shall see below, situations characterized by a high degree of autonomy of theoretical economics present certain difficulties for the application of the MSRP method of appraisal in economics. Before proceeding to examine these difficulties, let us first recall how MSRP was able to explain why economics research may often be characterized by numerous theoretical developments which are accompanied by both a relatively small amount of empirical testing and a relatively small concern about either empirical confirmations or empirical refutations.

Thus, as we saw in the previous chapter, such a high degree of autonomy of theoretical economics arises from the fact that the positive heuristic of a research programme is capable of generating theoretical developments almost completely independently of empirical testing. Consequently, while the positive heuristic continues to generate new theories, and while the empirical testing of these theories lags considerably behind their generation (due, for example, to the lack of suitable, readily available data), economics research will inevitably be characterized by numerous theoretical developments which are largely unaccompanied by empirical testing.

Now that we have MSRP's explanation of why a high degree of

autonomy of theoretical economics is to some extent *inevitable*, we shall proceed not only to note some of the *benefits* and *costs* of such autonomy, but also to note what guidance (if any) MSRP provides for situations where the costs of such autonomy exceed the benefits.

Benefits of theoretical autonomy

One important benefit of theoretical autonomy, according to MSRP, is that a period of theoretical autonomy may often be *necessary* in order to ensure that important breakthroughs (that is, breakthroughs embodying considerable theoretical and empirical progress) are achieved. To appreciate this point, let us first recall how the positive heuristic of the microeconomic research programme (discussed in Chapter 5) advised economics researchers to analyse the economic situation under consideration by constructing a series of ever more complicated theories. In other words, the analysis is to commence with theories which are deliberate simplifications of reality. Subsequently, as the research programme develops, these idealizations are to be replaced by increasingly sophisticated, and hopefully more realistic, theories.

Given this situation, note that as economics researchers progress through this succession of theories, moving from simple theories to more complex theories, they often will not require empirical refutations to tell them that these simple theories need to be modified or replaced. Rather, the positive heuristic will often have already informed them of this. Also, note that since many of these early idealizations may take the form of empirically *untestable* theories, it may not even be possible to expose these early idealizations to empirical testing. Finally, note that such a period of theoretical autonomy, characterized by a succession of untested and often untestable theories, presents no cause for alarm to MSRP. Rather, MSRP not only explicitly recognizes that important breakthroughs may only be achieved after many years of extensive theoretical work, but also it sees a period of theoretical autonomy as an integral part of the process of achieving such breakthroughs.

In other words, it is during this period of theoretical autonomy that the process of extensive refinement and improvement of untestable idealizations takes place and, in turn, it is out of this process that more sophisticated testable theories emerge. Hence, according to MSRP, to require only empirically testable versions of theories during this period is to endanger the very process by which significant breakthroughs are usually achieved. Similarly, according to MSRP, if too much attention were paid to anomalies, during this period of theoretical autonomy, this also could endanger the growth of economic knowledge.

A further, related, benefit of theoretical autonomy occurs in situations where economics researchers are considering whether certain theories, which have only been (sucessfully) exposed to a very small amount of empirical testing (for example, due to the lack of an historical data series), are suitable guides to economic policy-making. In such situations, rather than wait until more extensive empirical testing can take place, economics researchers can investigate the suitability of such theories by comparing their consequences or predictions with the consequences or predictions of more sophisticated (and hopefully more realistic) theories.

Thus, by making such *theoretical* comparisons, the sensitivity of the predictions of the initial theories to changes in the specification of these theories (resulting, for example, from the insertion of certain additional variables so as to make the theories more realistic) can be assessed and this, in turn, will provide useful insight into the suitability of these theories for policy guidance. In other words, such theoretical autonomy, or theoretical development which is independent of empirical testing, can provide an important means of investigating the adequacy of existing poorly-tested theories (even though this theoretical development consists of theories which either have not yet been empirically tested or may be empirically untestable in their present form).

Costs of theoretical autonomy

While the above paragraphs indicate certain ways in which theoretical autonomy may be beneficial to the growth of economic knowledge, it is also important to note that in other ways the autonomy of theoretical economics may be detrimental to the growth of economic knowledge.

For example, there is the very real danger that theoretical analysis may become an end in itself, so that increasing numbers of economics researchers not only become occupied with theoretical analysis but also combine this preoccupation with little or no concern as to whether the theoretical analysis will eventually lead to empirical progression. In other words, there is the danger that theoretical analysis may become increasingly divorced from reality instead of improving its correspondence with reality.

If this is the case, then not only will the growth of economic knowledge be hindered but also scarce research funds will be diverted away from research which is directed (as far as is possible) towards the goal of achieving *both* theoretical and empirical progression. Hence, instead of these research funds being spent on economics research which will advance economic knowledge, they will be spent on refining the finer points of existing theories in ways that are unlikely to produce both theoretical and empirical progression.

Difficulties of discerning the costs and benefits of theoretical autonomy

The preceding discussion, referring respectively to the benefits and costs of theoretical autonomy, helps to highlight the complex nature of economics research. On the one hand, while it must be recognized that a certain degree of autonomy of theoretical economics is both an inevitable and desirable feature of the growth of economic knowledge, on the other hand it must always be remembered that not all autonomous economics theorizing is beneficial to the growth of economic knowledge. Moreover, when we recognize the inevitable unpredictability of the outcome of economics research, it is by no means easy to discern which sections of economics theorizing are beneficial and which sections are not.

For example, many economists would quickly identify general equilibrium theorizing (which examines the interrelations among the constituent parts of an economic system) as an example of economics theorizing which is more concerned with refining logical problems than improving its correspondence with reality or achieving empirical application. Yet we must be very careful when making such identifications.

In particular, it is important to note that we would expect some economics theorizing to be directed towards an investigation of the interrelations among the constituent parts of an economic system. Also it should be noted that general equilibrium theorists have made many attempts to improve the correspondence of their theories with reality. Finally, it should be noted that important empirical applications have emerged from general equilibrium theorizing.

Thus, for example, general equilibrium theorizing has led to the development of input-output analysis which (by permitting empirical measurements of the interrelations in an economy and hence, in turn, enabling researchers to provide detailed empirical predictions of how changes in any one sector of the economy affect other sectors) has proved to be extremely valuable in numerous empirical applications throughout the world. In addition to this, the empirical application of even more sophisticated general equilibrium analysis has enabled economics researchers to obtain detailed empirical answers to important questions such as 'what are the static economic effects of the United Kingdom joining the European Economic Community?', *prior* to the United Kingdom joining the EEC (for example, see Miller [1971], and Miller and Spencer [1977], for the first application of computable models of general equilibrium).

The above examples of the important, and extremely useful, empirical applications that have emerged from general equilibrium theorizing make it very clear how cautious we have to be in appraising theoretical economics. Many economists have criticized general equilibrium theorists for constructing theories that are nothing more than very extreme idealizations of the real economy, and then spending excessive time refining these idealizations in ways that do little to enhance their correspondence with reality. Yet it has been the theoretical analysis of these very same idealizations which has led to the important empirical applications mentioned above. In other words, what may first appear to be fruitless theorizing may, in fact, be the prelude to exciting empirical applications and substantial growth in economic knowledge.

7.4 TOO HIGH A DEGREE OF THEORETICAL AUTONOMY IN CURRENT ECONOMICS?

While we have indicated the need for caution in assessing whether a high degree of autonomy of theoretical economics is beneficial or detrimental to the growth of economic knowledge, it must also be recognized that many economists are seriously concerned about the current state of economics research. Such economists feel that economics is currently characterized by an unhealthily high degree of autonomy of theoretical economics and an unhealthily low amount of empirical analysis. Consequently, they feel that so much theoretical analysis (which they consider to be mainly based on theories which are very extreme idealizations of real economic situations), accompanied not only by so little empirical analysis but also by such a low concern for empirical analysis, must inevitably lead to the costs of such theoretical autonomy exceeding the benefits. Hence they are concerned that the current state of economics research is detrimental to the growth of economic knowledge.

This concern, they argue, is supported by the fact that economics research articles which concentrate on mathematical economics and the finer points of economic theory are occupying an increasingly prominent place in economics journals, while articles which are more empirically-oriented or policy-oriented are occupying correspondingly less space. Moreover, they argue, when it is recognized that this research bias is increasingly accompanied by a corresponding bias in the education of both undergraduate and graduate economists, then it is even more likely that not only will economics research continue to have this unhealthy bias, but also the growth of economic knowledge will be hindered (for example, see Leontief [1982]).

An important difference between theorizing in economics and theorizing in physics

The above concern must be given serious consideration, especially when we recognize that theorizing in economics differs in at least one important respect from theorizing in a subject such as physics. Thus, for example, while there is a high degree of theoretical autonomy in physics, it is constructive to note that this theorizing is subject to important *constraints* which, in turn, tend to enhance the correspondence of this theorizing with reality.

To appreciate this point, let us first note that the growth of knowledge in physics has been characterized by the generation of a very large number of theories which, despite the most rigorous and extensive empirical testing, have not only remained unrefuted for a very long period of time but have also consistently continued to manifest an exceptionally high degree of predictive accuracy. Consequently, although 'higher-level' theorizing in physics enjoys a considerable degree of autonomy, this theorizing is constrained in the sense that its explanations must be generally consistent with the remarkable empirical success of 'lower-level' theories in physics.

The situation in economics is, however, almost the complete opposite of that in physics in the sense that economics, unfortunately, has a relative paucity of such empirically successful theories. This, in turn, means that economics does not possess the important check that such empirically successful theories provide and, consequently, theorizing in economics is more exposed to the danger of becoming seriously divorced from economic reality.

Important constraints on theorizing in economics

However, while it is important to note that theorizing in economics is not constrained in the same way as theorizing in physics, it is also important to note that there are other influences which tend to enhance the correspondence of economics theorizing with reality. In particular, since government and industry are constantly looking for both theoretical and empirical analysis to aid their policy-making decisions with regard to a very wide range of current policy-issues, this tends to exert an exceedingly important influence on economics theorizing. Not only does it mean that a large amount of economics theorizing is specifically directed towards solving current economic policy problems, but it also means that economics researchers are strongly encouraged to provide empirical support for their proposed solutions.

Consequently, when one remembers that a constant flow of research funds is being provided by government and industry in order to finance specific research projects, then we would expect this specific funding to operate as an important constraint ensuring that a considerable amount of research activity has either an empirical, policy-oriented character or an empirical, specific-problem-solving character. In other words, we would expect this constraint to help substantially in ensuring that economics researchers are constantly concerned that theoretical analysis should be quickly followed by empirical testing and, hopefully, empirical progress.

While the preceding paragraphs indicate that economics theorizing is constrained in some degree towards enhancing its correspondence with reality, many economists still feel that these constraints are inadequate to prevent the costs of theoretical autonomy exceeding its benefits and, therefore, feel that these constraints are inadequate to prevent theoretical autonomy from hindering the growth of economic knowledge. In addition, many of these economists also feel that there is too high a degree of theoretical autonomy in current economics.

However, as noted in Section 7.3, it is by no means easy to

discern whether or not the present degree of theoretical autonomy in economics is beneficial or detrimental to the growth of economic knowledge. Consequently, rather than try to assess the costs and benefits of the present degree of theoretical autonomy in economics, we shall instead ask the following important question: now that we have seen how it is possible for a situation to arise where the costs of theoretical autonomy exceed its benefits, what guidance does MSRP offer economics researchers so as to enable them to avoid such a situation of harmful theoretical autonomy? In other words, given that there is the danger that an excessive amount of theorizing may have insufficient correspondence with reality, can MSRP offer any guidance that will prevent such a situation from emerging? Unfortunately, as we shall see in the next section, the answer is that MSRP has very little guidance to offer.

7.5 MSRP AND THE AVOIDANCE OF HARMFUL THEORETICAL AUTONOMY

Before proceeding to examine why MSRP has little guidance to offer economics researchers that will prevent a situation of harmful theoretical autonomy from emerging, let us first recall that MSRP permits various empirical refutations to be tolerated within a research programme as long as some theoretical and empirical progress is being made. Thus, as we saw in the previous chapter, the positive heuristic of a research programme will guide researchers to ignore temporarily (but still record) certain empirical refutations in the hope that they will be accommodated later via further theoretical progress. Hence, as long as some theoretical progress is taking place, and provided that this theoretical progress is followed by some 'intermittent' empirical progress, then MSRP appraises the research programme in question as progressive.

Note, in relation to the preceding paragraph, that while MSRP has an explicit rationale for only requiring some 'intermittent' empirical progress, the time period to which 'intermittent' refers has been deliberately left undefined by MSRP. Given the MSRP rationale for temporarily ignoring certain empirical refutations, and the obvious unpredictability of the outcome of economics research, it is not hard to see why 'intermittent' is not precisely defined. However, while it is not difficult to see why the meaning of 'intermittent' has been left rather open-ended, we must now examine whether this is a matter for concern. In proceeding to do so below, we shall first note two aspects of theoretical autonomy (involving, respectively, *testable* and *untestable* theories) which will be relevant to our discussion.

Theoretical autonomy and testable theories

As a starting point, let us suppose that there has been a rather lengthy period of theoretical autonomy during which not only have various empirical refutations and anomalies been ignored but also no empirical progress has been achieved (even though a small amount of empirical testing has been taking place). In addition, let us suppose that, during this period, there has been a relatively low concern about empirical testing, with the result that many testable theories remain as yet untested.

Given this situation, does this then mean that the theoretical developments made during this period are in danger of becoming less and less (rather than more and more) in correspondence with reality? The answer, according to MSRP, is not necessarily. If theoretical progress is continuously taking place throughout this period, then this means that each new theory produced during this period must contain additional novel *testable* predictions which (because of this *testability* requirement), in turn, means that each successive theory will possess a higher degree of testability than its predecessor. This, it is hoped, will in turn eventually result in a closer correspondence with reality.

In other words, while there is no guarantee, it is hoped that the testability requirement will help to ensure that the series of theories produced during the period of theoretical autonomy will have an increasingly better correspondence with reality, and that this period of theoretical autonomy will eventually be followed by important theoretical and empirical progress.

Theoretical autonomy and untestable theories

Unfortunately, however, once we introduce *untestable* theories into the discussion, the danger of a decreased correspondence with reality becomes a very real possibility. To see this, let us now suppose that there has been a rather lengthy period of theoretical autonomy during which all the theoretical developments that have taken place (in accordance with the research programme's positive heuristic) have been in the form of increasingly sophisticated, *untestable* idealizations of the real economic situation.

Given this situation, we can note immediately that while theoretical development is taking place during this period, the additional predictions contained in each successive theory now take the form of *untestable* (rather than testable) predictions. This, in turn, means that the testability requirement, noted above, no longer operates to ensure that each successive theory will possess a higher degree of testability than its predecessor. Hence there is the very real possibility that each successive, untestable theory will become less (rather than more) in correspondence with reality.

In other words, while it is quite possible that the succession of untestable idealizations is converging towards a testable theory which has a very high correspondence with reality, there is no check in operation (akin to the above testability requirement) to help to ensure that this will, in fact, be the outcome. Thus, there is the danger that, during such periods of theoretical autonomy, economics research may generate a series of increasingly untestable theories that are also increasingly less (rather than increasingly more) in correspondence with reality. Consequently, during such periods of theoretical autonomy, there is the danger that the growth of economic knowledge will be hindered.

The danger of such a period of theoretical autonomy in economics research leading to a decline in the growth of economic knowledge becomes even greater when we remember that theoretical economics (in contrast to theoretical physics) is not constrained by many lower-level, empirically-successful theories towards a close correspondence with reality. Hence, instead of economics research being characterized by a movement from simple, untestable idealizations to increasingly realistic, testable theories, it is possible that such periods of theoretical autonomy may be characterized by a movement to increasingly unrealistic, untestable theories.

The inadequacy of MSRP's theoretical progress check

Now that we have seen that a period of theoretical autonomy may be characterized by theoretical developments involving *both* testable and untestable theories, we are in a position to appreciate the inadequacy of MSRP's theoretical progress check. In doing so, recall that while MSRP recognizes that the development of a research programme may be characterized by periods of theoretical autonomy, it only requires that 'some' theoretical progress be made in order for this theoretical development to be classed as theoretically progressive. But how little or how much is 'some'? How much theoretical development in the form of *untestable* theories is permitted before *testable* theories are required to be produced?

The answer, unfortunately, is not supplied by MSRP. Consequently, MSRP has very little, if any, guidance to offer economics researchers that will prevent a situation of harmful theoretical autonomy from emerging. In other words, while the MSRP requirement of 'some' theoretical progress provides a check that will help to ensure that some testable theories are produced and this, in turn, will hopefully enhance the correspondence of these theories with reality (via the influence of the testability requirement), the very imprecision of this check means that it offers very little protection against the emergence of harmful theoretical autonomy.

Hence, while MSRP accepts that periods of theoretical autonomy are not only an inevitable but also a desirable feature of the process by which significant theoretical breakthroughs are usually achieved, it does not provide the guidance that is necessary during such periods in order to prevent economics research from becoming less and less in correspondence with reality.

The inadequacy of MSRP's empirical progress check

Admittedly, since MSRP requires some 'intermittent' empirical progress, the requirement of empirical progress will eventually constrain economics researchers either to produce theories which are both empirically testable and empirically successful or, if this fails to take place, to recognize that the research programme in question is degenerating. But then, how long do we have to wait before this 'intermittent' check operates? Since no period of time is defined for 'intermittent', we may have to wait a very long time. Thus, for example, it may take a considerable length of time before it is recognized that the theoretical developments (made in full accordance with the research programme's positive heuristic) which have been taking place are not progressive modifications of the protective belt, but instead are *ad hoc* modifications produced by a degenerating research programme.

Note, in addition, that MSRP's 'intermittent' empirical progress check may operate too slowly not only in situations where the theoretical developments involve both testable and untestable theories, but also in situations where *testable*, but as yet *untested*, theories are involved. Thus, in situations where theoretical progress may be taking place, in the sense that successive theories each contain empirically testable predictions that are additional their respective predecessors, too long a period may lapse before these theories are tested and hence before it is recognized that these additional predictions are not empirically confirmed. This possibility is especially likely in periods of theoretical autonomy that are characterized by little or no concern about the urgency of empirical testing.

Moreover, since very little empirical testing and hence very little empirical refutation (or confirmation) is taking place during such periods of theoretical autonomy, this means that the process of empirical testing and refutation is only permitted to operate as a very minor stimulus enhancing the correspondence of successive theories with reality. This, in turn, reinforces the danger of such periods of theoretical autonomy hindering the growth of economic knowledge.

The inadequacy of MSRP's 'intermittent' empirical progress check becomes even more obvious when we remember that MSRP permits researchers to overlook certain empirical refutations in the hope that they will be accommodated by later modifications of the protective belt. To the extent that this takes place too often (and this excessive overlooking of refutations is only too likely since MSRP does not make clear how the programme's positive heuristic tells researchers which refutations should be ignored and which should be heeded), then the 'intermittent' empirical progress check will be weakened even further. Consequently, even if the testability requirement is fulfilled in such situations (and hence successive theories are constrained to be hopefully in closer correspondence with reality), the delay in testing these theories, together with the ignoring of their refutation, may seriously delay the realization that the research programme is degenerating.

Also, even after the MSRP check of 'intermittent' empirical progress has operated to class a research programme as degenerating, MSRP recognizes that economics researchers may continue to attempt to revive this research programme instead of either moving to an alternative research programme or starting to construct a new one. Consequently, if this revival attempt takes a long period of time, either before it succeeds in making a progressive comeback or before economics researchers recognize that such a comeback is highly unlikely ever to be achieved, then it is possible that there may be a very long period of fruitless economics research.

The above discussion clearly shows that MSRP has little guidance to offer economics researchers that will prevent situations of harmful theoretical autonomy from emerging. This, in turn, helps us to see just how limited the MSRP method of appraisal is. While it does provide a day-to-day method of appraisal for situations where researchers are only dealing with both *testable and tested* theories (in the sense that these theories can be appraised as theoretically and empirically progressive, or otherwise, at a given point in time), it does not provide a precise method of appraisal in situations which also involve both *untested* (though testable) and *untestable* theories. In the latter situations (which normally characterize day-to-day economics research), MSRP can only provide a *retrospective* appraisal of a research programme. Consequently, the MSRP appraisal of a research programme at a given point in time is far from precise.

(For a discussion of the difficulties associated with attempts to introduce other supplementary appraisal criteria such as the logical consistency, elegance, extensibility, generality and simplicity of theories, see Caldwell [1982], pp. 231-5; Newton-Smith [1981], pp. 226-35 and Watkins [1984], Chapter 4.)

However, while the above discussion indicates the limitations of the MSRP method of appraisal, it must be remembered that (given the obvious unpredictability of the outcome of economics research) it is rather unrealistic to expect a methodology of economics to be such that it provides a set of precise rules, which ensure that economics researchers will always take the correct steps when approaching and appraising their research activity. Furthermore, it should be recognized that, despite its lack of precise appraisal criteria, MSRP not only represents an important attempt to provide a methodology which is an improvement over falsificationism (and, in turn, over inductivism and instrumentalism), but it also provides important insight into those features of economics research activity which are likely to enhance or to hinder the growth of economic knowledge.

7.6 SHOULD MSRP PAY MORE ATTENTION TO EMPIRICAL REFUTATIONS?

In this section, we shall proceed to ask whether MSRP could be improved by requiring economics researchers to pay more attention both to empirical testing and to empirical refutations, while still accepting the particular research programme's hard core. In other words, if MSRP required economics researchers to take both empirical testing and empirical refutations more seriously, would this provide an important stimulus to the generation of protective belt modifications that have a closer correspondence with reality?

On the one hand, the answer to the above question would appear to be yes. Thus, it can be argued that if researchers take empirical refutations seriously (as falsificationism would require), they will try to modify the research programme's protective belt so as to overcome the specific problems these refutations pose, and hence the resultant modifications will be kept in fairly close correspondence with reality.

However, on the other hand, if we do this, are we not forgetting the important MSRP rationale for temporarily ignoring (though recording) certain empirical refutations and thus endangering the very process by which important theoretical breakthroughs are usually achieved? Not necessarily—provided economics research (within a *given* research programme) is characterized by a division of labour. Hence, if one group of economics researchers proceed in the usual MSRP manner (ignoring certain empirical refutations in the hope that these will be accommodated by later modifications of the research programme's protective belt), and the rest proceed in a falsificationist manner (taking not only testability and empirical refutations seriously but also the urgency of testing untested theories as soon as possible), then this division of labour should reduce the research risks and, hopefully, enhance the growth of economic knowledge.

It should be noted, however, that while the above suggestion (found in Musgrave [1973]), to incorporate more falsificationism within MSRP, does represent (in our opinion) a methodological improvement over the original MSRP, it fails to answer many important detailed questions. For example, what percentage of economics researchers and research funds should be allocated to each type of research activity so as best to enhance the growth of economic knowledge? Despite these difficulties, we feel that the requirement of more falsificationism within MSRP would provide a useful, corrective influence on research activity in economics which, in turn, should hopefully enhance the growth of economic knowledge.

The difficulty of obtaining conclusive empirical results

It is also important to note that not only does the requirement of more falsificationism within MSRP leave open questions about the division of labour in economics research, but also it may often fail to provide the conclusive empirical results that one would desire. The reason for this is simply that economics research is faced with the formidable task of investigating a highly complex subject matter. Thus not only has economics research to face the difficulties of investigating a relatively large number of relevant variables in each research situation, but also it has to face the additional difficulties that arise from the fact that these variables (and their interrelations not only with each other but also with other variables) are changing through time. Moreover, this highly complex, changing subject matter means that even empirically successful theories must be constantly retested over time.

Consequently, when we take into account the complexity of economic systems, plus the associated institutional changes, plus finally the much greater difficulty (or virtual impossibility) of controlled experiments in economics, it is not surprising that it is extremely difficult for economics researchers to achieve decisive empirical results. Thus, rather than economics being characterized by clear-cut empirical testing, economics researchers are faced with the difficulty that empirical confirmations and empirical refutations cannot easily be unambiguously interpreted as representing, respectively, either the confirmation or the refutation of any theory under test.

The complex, changing subject matter of economics and the related difficulty of obtaining conclusive empirical results, despite heroic attempts by econometricians to improve empirical testing in economics, helps to explain why economics (in contrast, for example, to physics) has an extreme paucity of theories which (after rigorous testing) have remained unrefuted for a long period of time and which consistently manifest an exceptionally high degree of predictive accuracy. However, despite these difficulties facing the requirement of a greater empirical emphasis within MSRP, we feel that this greater empirical emphasis should nonetheless be encouraged (via the division of research labour discussed above), and persevered with (more so than it is in the current state of economics research), in order to enhance both the correspondence of economics research with reality and, hopefully, the growth of economic knowledge.

(Note that the argument of the preceding two paragraphs constitutes a further criticism of falsificationism. In other words, for falsificationism to work as a viable methodology, it requires that empirical tests provide unambiguous results of either confirmation or refutation. Since, to an unfortunately large extent, this requirement is not fulfilled in the current state of economics, then falsificationism cannot be readily applied to economics.)

Before ending this chapter with a summary, note that Chapter 8 contains a further examination of the implications of adopting MSRP in economics. In particular, Chapter 8 extends the discussion of this chapter to include the case of competing research programmes.

7.7 SUMMARY

The above discussion has indicated how the adoption of MSRP would provide economics researchers with suggestions as to how both to approach and appraise their research activity.

Thus, as we have seen, once economics researchers have adopted MSRP as a suitable methodology, they will approach their research activity with the realization that it is part of a research programme. This, in turn, implies that they will not only view the relevant research programme as an organized structure of linked groupings of hypotheses, but they will also be able to make a clear-cut distinction between hard core and protective belt hypotheses.

In addition, once economics researchers have adopted MSRP, we would expect them to follow the negative heuristic advice that the hard core of the research programme is not to be rejected or modified during the development of the programme. Also, we would expect them to be able to identify (and follow the advice of) the positive heuristic of the research programme, not only with its research agenda and its guidance about how to develop and modify the protective belt hypotheses, but also with its guidance about how to cope with logical and empirical difficulties that arise in the development of the programme.

Lastly, once economics researchers have adopted MSRP, not only will they approach their research activity in the way just described, but also they will appraise the development of the relevant research programme as either progressive or degenerating depending upon whether or not it is both theoretically and empirically progressive.

However, as we have seen, the adoption of MSRP may not be quite so straightforward as it appears. For example, as we have noted in Section 7.2, the difficulty of drawing a clear-cut distinction between hard core and protective belt hypotheses essentially means that the MSRP method of appraisal can only be applied to well-articulated, mature research programmes where the hard core/protective belt distinction is clearly recognizable. In cases where this distinction is not clear-cut, a modified form of MSRP could, however, be utilized.

As noted in Section 7.2, the possibility of using a modified form of MSRP would tend to suggest that we should abandon the hard core/protective belt distinction altogether when appraising research programmes in economics. However, as also noted in Section 7.2, it is our opinion that there is good reason for retaining this distinction and, consequently, we shall examine this point in more detail in Chapter 8.

A further difficulty facing the adoption of MSRP may arise in certain periods of theoretical autonomy in economics. Hence, although MSRP provides us with important insight into the costs and benefits associated with periods of theoretical autonomy in economics, it has very little guidance to offer economics researchers that will prevent situations of harmful theoretical autonomy from emerging. While MSRP does provide a day-to-day method of appraisal for situations involving testable and tested theories, it does not provide a precise method of appraisal in (the not uncommon) situations involving both untested (though testable) and untestable theories. Consequently, as noted in Section 7.5, the MSRP appraisal of a research programme at a given point in time is far from precise.

As noted in Section 7.3, some of MSRP's inadequacy arises from the sheer difficulty of discerning the costs and benefits of theoretical autonomy in economics. However, as noted in Section 7.6, since some of MSRP's inadequacy also arises from its (deliberately) loosely defined requirement of empirical progress, we briefly examined the question of whether MSRP should pay more attention to empirical refutations. In doing so, we concluded that, despite the difficulties of obtaining conclusive empirical results in economics research, this greater empirical emphasis would constitute an important improvement, to the MSRP method of appraisal, for combating the difficulties faced by economics researchers. Thus, as noted in Section 7.6, it is our opinion that this greater empirical emphasis (accompanied by the division of research labour discussed in Section 7.6) would enchance both the correspondence of economics research with reality and, hopefully, the growth of economic knowledge.

Finally, while the discussion in this chapter has indicated the limitations of the MSRP method of appraisal, we noted that (given the obvious unpredictability of the outcome of economics research) it is rather unrealistic to expect a methodology of economics to be such that it provides a set of precise rules which ensure that economics researchers will always take the correct steps when approaching and appraising their research activity. In particular, we feel it is important to note just how extremely difficult it is to provide a methodology that will solve the problems of appraising or selecting theories in economics. Not only is the appraisal of research activity necessarily complex in itself, but when we add to this the complex subject matter of economics plus the difficulties facing empirical work in economics, we can see that the whole question of theory appraisal in economics is exceedingly complex.

Against this background, we feel that it is to the credit of MSRP that it not only provides us with important insight into this complex research situation, but that it also has succeeded in providing important (though, not surprisingly, limited) guidance as to how we should approach the difficult task of theory appraisal in economics. Also, we feel that it should be recognized that, despite its lack of precise appraisal criteria, MSRP not only represents an important attempt to provide a methodology which is an improvement over falsificationism (and, in turn, over inductivism and instrumentalism), but it also provides important insight into those features of economics research activity which are likely to enhance or hinder the growth of economic knowledge.

References for further reading

Criticism and discussion of MSRP can be found in Berkson [1976]; Chalmers [1982], Chapters 9-11; Cross [1982a]; Hands [1979], [1984] and [1985b]; Koertge [1971] and [1978]; McMullin [1978]; Musgrave [1973], [1976] and [1978]; and Rosenberg [1986].

8 Implications of Adopting MSRP in Economics—II

In this chapter we shall continue our examination of the implications of adopting MSRP in economics. In particular, we shall extend the discussion of Chapter 7 to include the case of competing research programmes.

8.1 MSRP AND THE APPRAISAL OF COMPETING RESEARCH PROGRAMMES

As noted in Chapter 6, the relative merits of competing research programmes are to be evaluated by reference to their respective degrees of explanatory power or progressiveness. In other words, in such comparisons, if one research programme is capable not only of explaining the previous successes of a rival research programme but also of providing additional novel explanatory content which has been empirically confirmed then, according to MSRP, it is regarded as being superior to its rival. Also, as noted in Chapter 6, the evaluation of the relative merits of competing research programmes is to include a comparison of each research programme's heuristic strength. Hence, according to MSRP, a more progressive, heuristically stronger research programme is regarded as superior to a less progressive, heuristically weaker research programme.

However, while the preceding paragraph would appear to suggest that MSRP can be readily used to compare rival research programmes, it must be recognized that such comparison is very problematic. As noted in Chapter 7, it is very difficult to appraise precisely a research programme at a given point in time. This difficulty arises from the fact that such an appraisal necessarily involves not just the appraisal of *tested* theories but also the appraisal of *untested* (though testable) and *untestable* theories. Consequently, when we also note how difficult it is to gauge precisely the heuristic power of a research programme at a given point in time, then we can see that the appraisal of a research programme and, in turn, its comparison with other research programmes is far from straightforward.

To this already complex picture, we must also add the commensurability problem (noted in Chapter 6) which arises in situations where one research programme (denoted as RP_2) contains some, but not all, of the empirically-confirmed explanatory content of its rival (denoted as RP_1), and where RP_2 contains an additional amount of empirically-confirmed explanatory content not contained in RP_1. Clearly, in such situations, where a loss as well as a gain in explanatory content is involved, the comparison of research programmes will be difficult, even though MSRP does provide guidance for such comparisons (see Section 6.5).

Finally, as we shall explain in more detail below, the commensurability problem is further complicated by the fact that the hard cores of rival research programmes contain statements which have very different ethical, social and political implications.

In order to highlight the above difficulties in comparing research programmes and to see what insight or guidance MSRP provides in the face of such difficulties, we shall now proceed to identify what we consider to be the major research programmes in economics and to indicate where, in our estimation, the major problems of commensurability are located.

8.2 MAJOR RESEARCH PROGRAMMES IN ECONOMICS

When we start to look for major research programmes in economics, which attempt to explain the various economic aspects of capitalist economies, two obvious candidates spring quickly to mind: the 'orthodox' economics research programme (containing the numerous microeconomic and macroeconomic theories which are predominantly taught in western universities, polytechnics and schools) and the 'Marxist' economics research programme (containing both Marx's economics and subsequent developments of

Marx's economic analysis). As we shall explain in more detail below, the *orthodox* and *Marxist* research programmes have very different, distinctive hard cores and positive heuristics which, in turn, complicate the comparison of these two research programmes.

Before proceeding to provide an outline of some important features of Marx's economics, and then comparing the Marxist and orthodox research programmes, we must first remove the apparent inconsistency between our previous 'microeconomics research programme' and the orthodox research programme. In other words, we must clarify why, in Chapter 5, we referred to the microeconomics research programme as a research programme in its own right, yet in the preceding paragraph we have somehow incorporated the microeconomics research programme within the orthodox research programme.

The orthodox research programme and its subprogrammes

To remove the apparent inconsistency between the microeconomics research programme and the orthodox research programme, note that we view the orthodox research programme as a *single* programme which, in turn, contains several *subprogrammes* within it (see also Archibald [1979], p.309). Hence, given this view, the microeconomics research programme can now be seen as a *subprogramme* within the wider orthodox research programme, with the orthodox research programme not only having the same hard core as the microeconomics research programme, but also incorporating the microeconomics research programme's positive heuristic within a somewhat larger positive heuristic. Moreover, as we shall see below, this view also enables us to define macroeconomic research activity as a subprogramme within the wider orthodox research programme.

Further to appreciate how we view the orthodox research programme, note first that the hard core of the orthodox research programme, and hence the hard core underlying *both* (orthodox) microeconomic and (orthodox) macroeconomic research activity, is envisaged as being composed of the following four basic assumptions or hypotheses (which were introduced and explained in Section 5.3): *individualism*, *rationality*, *private property rights*, and a *market economy*.

Having presented the hard core of the orthodox research programme as identical to the hard core of the microeconomics subprogramme, we must now indicate why we also consider this to be the hard core underlying the macroeconomics subprogramme.

To do this, note that while introductory economics textbooks may define macroeconomics as the study of the overall economic aggregates of the economy, in contrast to microeconomics which may be defined as the study of individual economic units within the economy, more advanced macroeconomic analysis indicates that macroeconomic theory, in common with microeconomic theory, rests on propositions about the rational behaviour of individuals. This, in turn, explains why *individualism* and *rationality* can be regarded as hard core hypotheses in relation to macroeconomic analysis. Furthermore, since macroeconomic analysis also presupposes both *private property rights* and a *market economy*, we can see why the hypotheses of private property rights and a market economy can also be regarded as hard core hypotheses in relation to macroeconomic analysis.

With regard to the positive heuristic of the orthodox research programme, note that we view this positive heuristic as containing guidelines which economics researchers may use in *both* microeconomic and macroeconomic research activity.

In support of this view of the positive heuristic, note that not only do microeconomics and macroeconomics make extensive use of *equilibrium analysis*, *comparative-static analysis*, and *dynamic analysis*, but also in various areas of both microeconomics and macroeconomics we find that a *perfectly competitive market structure* has been assumed. Also, as researchers in macroeconomics have investigated the microeconomic foundations of their macroeconomic theories, considerable use has been made of *optimization analysis*. This, however, is not to deny that the positive heuristic of the orthodox research programme has certain guidelines for macroeconomics research that are distinctly different (at least in emphasis) from those for microeconomics research. Hence, for example, more emphasis may be put on working at an aggregate rather than a disaggregate level, on short-run analysis rather than long-run analysis, and on output adjustment rather than price adjustment.

Moreover, within the *macroeconomics subprogramme* of the orthodox research programme, specific areas of research (which we shall also refer to as subprogrammes in order not only to stress the programmatic aspect of the research activity but also to stress that this research activity is part of the wider orthodox research programme) may be identified by their distinctive positive heuristic guidelines.

For example, the basic *Keynesian* subprogramme could be identified by the following distinctive positive heuristic: 'explain changes in the levels of national income (or output) and employment in terms of changes in the level of aggregate expenditure' (see Cross [1982b], Chapters 3 and 4). Likewise, since basic monetarists explain changes in the price level in terms of prior changes in the stock of money, then the basic *monetarist* subprogramme could be identified by the following distinctive positive heuristic: 'explain sustained changes in the price level by sustained prior changes in the stock of money' (see Cross [1982b], Chapter 8).

Note, in each of these examples, that the distinctive positive heuristic will, in turn, give rise to a distinctive set of protective belt hypotheses. Hence each subprogramme will contain both a distinctive positive heuristic and a distinctive set of protective belt hypotheses. (Also, note that while other examples could be given (see Cross [1982b], Chapters 3–10), these two examples will suffice.)

In a similar fashion, specific areas of research within the *microeconomics subprogramme* of the orthodox research programme may be identified by their distinctive positive heuristic guidelines. For example, the research activity concerned with the analysis of business firms may be divided into subprogrammes with distinctive positive heuristics such as: 'explain changes in the firm's level of output in response to certain changes in its situation (such as changes in the demand for its product, changes in the rate of profits tax, and changes in a lump sum tax), under the assumption that the entrepreneur's goal is *profit maximization*', and 'explain changes in the firm's level of output, in response to the same changes in its situation, under the assumption that the entrepreneur's goal is *revenue maximization* (subject to the constraint that he earns some specified minimum amount of profits)'.

Note, in each of these examples, that the distinctive positive heuristic will, in turn, give rise to a distinctive set of protective belt hypotheses. (Also, note that other examples could be given both from research related to the business firm and from other areas of research within the microeconomics subprogramme.)

It is important to note, however, that while various subprogrammes may be identified via their distinctive positive heuristics (and, consequently, will contain distinctive protective belt hypotheses), each of these subprogrammes also makes considerable use of identical analytical techniques and methods of solving problems. In other words, they all draw (to varying extents) on the extensive positive heuristic of the 'parent' orthodox research programme.

Also, note that each of the subprogrammes (whether we are thinking of a subprogramme at the microeconomics subprogramme level or a subprogramme at a much lower level, such as the subprogrammes concerned with the analysis of the business firm) *implies* the hard core of the 'parent' orthodox research programme. Consequently, when the microeconomics research programme is now seen as a subprogramme (namely, the microeconomics subprogramme) implying the hard core of the 'parent' orthodox research programme, then the above-mentioned apparent inconsistency between the microeconomics research programme and the orthodox research programme disappears.

Finally, note that the level at which a subprogramme is to be defined has been deliberately left flexible in order to suit the situation under consideration. If, for example, we wish to compare different approaches to the analysis of business firms, then we can define and compare subprogrammes at this level. Similarly, if we wish to compare orthodox macroeconomics with Marx's macroeconomics, then we must define and compare the respective subprogrammes at the level appropriate for this (noting, in the process, that the orthodox macroeconomics subprogramme will imply the hard core of the orthodox research programme, whereas Marx's macroeconomics subprogramme will imply the hard core of the Marxist research programme).

The appraisal of subprogrammes

Since each subprogramme of the orthodox research programme not only implies the hard core of the 'parent' orthodox research programme but also contains its own distinctive protective belt, then each of these subprogrammes can be appraised via the MSRP appraisal criteria of progressiveness and heuristic strength. In addition, rival subprogrammes within the orthodox research programme, such as the basic Keynesian and basic monetarist subprogrammes, can also be compared via the MSRP appraisal criteria.

However, while MSRP can be used to compare rival subprogrammes within the orthodox research programme, it should be noted that such comparison is by no means straightforward. For example, just as it is very difficult to appraise a research programme at a given point in time, it is also very difficult to appraise a subprogramme precisely at a given point in time. This difficulty arises from the fact that such an appraisal necessarily involves not just the appraisal of tested theories but also the appraisal of untested (though testable) and untestable theories. When we add to this the difficulty of precisely gauging the heuristic strength of a subprogramme, plus any content-comparison difficulties, it is evident that the comparison of subprogrammes is very problematic.

Now that we have clarified our definition of the orthodox research programme and its various subprogrammes, we shall proceed to provide a brief outline of certain important features of Marx's economics in order that we may appreciate the essential differences between the orthodox economics research programme and the Marxist economics research programme.

8.3 MARX'S ECONOMICS: AN OUTLINE OF SOME IMPORTANT FEATURES

In Marx's analysis of capitalism, a labour theory of value plays an important role. Thus, according to Marx's labour theory of value, the value of a commodity is determined by the amount of socially necessary labour time embodied in its production (with 'socially necessary' meaning under normal production conditions with the average degree of skills and work intensity prevailing at that point in time). Note, however, that this value includes not only the labour time directly involved in producing the commodity, but also the past labour time embodied in the amounts of raw materials, machinery and plant used up in producing the commodity.

The structure of property rights also plays an important role in Marx's economic analysis. Hence, in Marx's analysis, while the capitalists are presented as having private property rights over the means of production (that is, the machinery, raw materials and plant), the workers are viewed as having no property rights over the means of production. Given this structure of property rights, the capitalist who owns the means of production will then hire workers in the market with a view to producing commodities for exchange.

At this point in his analysis, Marx stresses that what the workers sell in the market is their *labour power* (that is, their potential capacity for productive activity). Since labour power is viewed as a commodity, then its value is determined (like that of any other commodity) by the socially necessary labour time embodied in its production. In other words, the value of labour power is the amount of socially necessary labour time embodied in commodities (such as food, clothing, housing, education, training, etc) that are necessary not only to support the worker and his family but also to reproduce the labour power, under the prevailing technical and social conditions.

Once the worker has sold his labour power to the capitalist at its (historically and socially determined) value, then the capitalist has control over the worker's labour power in the sense that the capitalist decides how the worker's capacity for productive activity will be utilized in the production process. In addition, the commodities produced by the application of the worker's labour power are the property of the capitalist.

Let us now assume that, in order to produce a commodity, a capitalist buys labour power in the market at a value of 30 labour hours (with this value of labour power being equal to the socially necessary labour time embodied in the commodities that are necessary to maintain and reproduce the labour power). Also, let us assume that, in order to produce the commodity, workers are made to work 50 hours. Finally, let us assume that the raw materials, machinery and plant used up in producing the commodity have a value of 40 labour hours. Given these assumptions, Marx's labour theory of value indicates that the value of the commodity produced is 50+40=90 labour hours. In other words, while the capitalist has only paid a value of 30+40=70 labour hours for the inputs required to produce the commodity, the value of the commodity is 90 labour hours. Hence, there is *surplus value* of 90-70=20 labour hours (defined, in value terms, as the difference between the value of the commodity and the value of the inputs used up in the production process).

It is important to note, in the above account, that the value of raw materials, machinery and plant used up in the production process is simply transferred in full to the value of the commodity being produced. Hence, while these means of production are clearly productive (in that they increase physical production), they do not create value in the process of production. Rather, they merely pass on their value. Consequently, in Marx's analysis, it is labour power which not only produces value to replace itself (the 30 labour hours in the above example) but also creates surplus value (the 20 labour hours in the above example). In other words, surplus value is created in the production process by the productive activity of *unpaid labour*.

Although there appears to be no exploitation, in the sense that all labour is paid labour (receiving the 30 labour hours in the above example), exploitation takes place in reality in the sense that workers are made to work 50 hours (in the above example) but are only paid a fraction (the 30 labour hours) of the value produced (the 30+20=50 labour hours) by the utilization of this 50 hours of labour power.

This exploitation, or the appropriation of surplus value by the capitalist from the workers, gives rise to *class conflict*. Thus, in Marx's analysis of capitalism, class conflict arises directly out of the capitalist production process, with the capitalist class's appropriation of the surplus value being crucially related to the structure of ownership and non-ownership of the means of production that characterize the capitalist production process.

This class antagonism will (according to Marx), in turn, operate as a driving force leading to social revolution and to change in social forms of production, property relationships, and the distribution of goods. Hence, according to Marx, the workers will eventually bring about the overthrow of capitalism which, in turn, will put an end to all class distinctions and to all forms of exploitation. In particular, in order to secure this post-revolution situation, the means of production will no longer be monopolized by the capitalists but instead will become social property. In other words, *private ownership* (or *private property rights*) will be replaced by *social ownership* (or *social property rights*).

It is important to note that the foregoing brief outline excludes many other important features of Marx's economics, such as how Marx handles heterogeneous labour in his labour theory of value, competition between capitalists, capital accumulation by capitalists, how the capital accumulation process produces an 'industrial reserve army' of unemployed workers, how the industrial reserve army puts a downward pressure on wages, and details of the transition from capitalism to socialism and thus to communism.

However, while the above brief outline does not include these other features, the features of Marx's economics which have been highlighted will (together with the discussion following in Sections 8.4 and 8.5) enable us to pinpoint the distinctive differences between the Marxist research programme and the orthodox research programme. Hence, on the basis of the above outline, we can now proceed to a brief examination of the component parts of the Marxist economics research programme. (For further discussion of Marx's economics, see Fine [1984], Junakar [1982], and Howard and King [1985].)

8.4 THE HARD CORE OF THE MARXIST RESEARCH PROGRAMME

The hard core of the Marxist research programme is very different from that of the orthodox research programme:

The social nature of individual economic agents: While Marx's analysis of capitalism deals with the behaviour of individual economic agents, he maintains that one cannot deal with the individual economic agent in abstraction from his social and historical setting. Consequently, Marx's analysis, in contrast to orthodox economic analysis, stresses the *social* nature of the individual economic agent within a specific historical setting.

However, this does not mean that society is viewed as an entity distinct from the individual economic agents or that the individual economic agent is viewed as a product of society. Rather, Marx's social image of the individual economic agent means that there is an integration and interaction of individual and society in his economic analysis, so that change in individual economic agents is thereby also change in society and change in social circumstances is also change in individual economic agents (see Avineri [1968], pp. 86-95).

Rationality with a social dimension: The Marxist research programme, in common with the orthodox research programme, contains the basic assumption or hypothesis of *rationality*. However, the Marxist research programme views this assumption in a way that is distinctly different from that of the orthodox research programme. Thus, while this assumption embodies the requirement that economic agents make their economic calculations in a consistent way, this consistency of behaviour in the Marxist analysis is viewed as taking place in a historically specific social context.

Hence, given a particular problem-situation, rational behaviour is taken as that behaviour which is appropriate to this given situation in the sense that individual economic agents act in a way that is consistent with their respective social relations (and therefore with their respective class positions as defined by these social relations), with these social relations corresponding, in turn, to the historically specific economic structure (in our case mature capitalism) under consideration.

Property ownership as a social relation: The Marxist research programme also views the basic assumption or hypothesis of *private property rights* in a way that is distinctly different from that of the orthodox research programme.

In Marx's analysis of capitalism the means of production are monopolized as the private property of the capitalist class. In contrast, the working class are presented as having no property rights over the means of production. This particular structure of property ownership, in turn, not only defines a specific social relationship between the two classes, but also means that the production process has an important social character.

On the one hand, it is the worker's non-ownership of the means of production which compels him to sell his only asset, his labour power, to the capitalist. On the other hand, it is the capitalist's ownership of the means of production which not only leads him to buy the workers's labour power, but also empowers him to appropriate the surplus value created by the worker. In other words, the capitalist's ownership of property is not just simply viewed as an initial endowment of 'things' (such as buildings, machinery and raw materials) but rather as a *social relation* which, in turn, determines the social form of the production process.

Moreover, in Marx's analysis, since the structure of property ownership enables the capitalist not only to dominate the worker (via the former's ownership, and hence control, of the production process) but also to exploit the worker (by appropriating the surplus value), then the class antagonism, which arises directly out of the capitalist production process, can be crucially related to the specific structure of ownership and non-ownership of property that characterizes mature capitalism.

In contrast, the orthodox research programme generally assumes some initial structure of property ownership without attempting to analyse the specific *social* relationships which flow from this. Hence, in the orthodox research programme, property ownership is viewed essentially as ownership of 'things' (which may either be used in the production of further things or exchanged for other things), rather than as a social relation. Also, in contrast to Marx's analysis where the property rights have a *historical* character (since they are the property rights *specific* to mature capitalism), property rights in the orthodox research programme are *ahistorical* in character.

Social relationships between people lie beneath the market exchange of commodities: In the Marxist research programme, as in the orthodox research programme, a *market economy* is assumed. However, in Marx's analysis, the concept of exchange is very different from that of the orthodox research programme. Whereas in the latter exchange is simply a relationship between 'things' (with 'things' referring to the commodities which are exchanged via the market system, and where the commodities, in turn, refer not only to physical goods but also to labour time which workers sell as a good in the market), in Marx's analysis this relationship between things is simultaneously a relationship between people.

Thus, in Marx's analysis, the social character of production (that is, the social or class relationships which characterize the capitalist production process) is expressed through the exchange of commodities. Consequently, according to Marx, it is necessary to probe beneath the 'appearance' of mere exchange of commodities in the market to the 'reality' of social relationships between people.

In his view, it is only by going beneath market exchange to the social form of production (and hence to the class relationships which characterize the production process) that exchange in a capitalist economy can be adequately analysed. Hence, in his analysis, the emphasis is heavily placed on the social production relations rather than on the phenomenon of market exchange. Moreover, since the social form of production lying beneath market exchange is taken to be that which is historically specific to mature capitalism, then exchange in Marx's analysis has a specific *historical* character as well as a *social* dimension.

Historical materialism: The growth of the forces of production (defined as the physical means of production, such as machinery, raw materials and buildings, plus labour power) is given a primary explanatory role in Marx's economic analysis. Thus, while at a particular stage in the historical development of an economy there is both a correspondence and a compatibility between the forces of production and the social relations of production (with the latter, in linking productive forces and economic agents in the production process, against the specific background of economic ownership and non-ownership of the means of production, defining the class position of individual economic agents), the forces of production are given a dominant role. Hence, the forces of production are viewed as determining the social relations of production.

As the productive forces develop, they become incompatible with the existing social relations of production. Hence, rather than enhancing increased material production, the existing social relations now constitute an obstacle to the continued development of society's productive capacity. The growth of the productive forces is thus viewed as leading to a contradiction between the forces and relations of production and therefore to class conflict. The intensification of this incompatibility and conflict is then regarded as a driving force which leads to the breakdown of the existing mode of production (defined as encompassing the technical nature of the productive process, the social relations of production and the attendant property relations), and to its replacement by another mode of production (with new social relations of production which better accommodate the expansion of society's productive capacity).

Since the above account, of how the growth of productive forces play a dominant role in Marx's economic analysis, is known as *historical materialism*, we must also explicitly include this materialist conception of history in the hard core of the Marxist research programme.

(For support for the view that the productive forces have the above dominant role, as opposed to the view that the social relations of production are primary or the view that the forces and relations are mutually determining, see Cohen [1978] and Shaw [1978]. For an alternative view see Levine and Wright [1980].)

The above discussion indicates the distinctive ways in which the hard core of the Marxist research programme differs, in our view, from the hard core of the orthodox research programme. Thus, in the hard core of the Marxist research programme, *individualism* is replaced by *the social nature of individual economic agents*, *rationality* is viewed as *rationality with a social dimension*, *private property rights* are viewed as a *social power relation*, and a *market economy* is viewed in terms of the *social relationships lying beneath the exchange of commodities*. In addition, the hard core of the Marxist research programme also contains a *materialist conception of history*, with the process of historical development involved being essentially viewed as *dialectical* in character.

It should be noted that the above discussion, together with the discussion of the hard core of the orthodox research programme (in Sections 8.2 and 5.3), does not attempt to provide an exhaustive characterization of the hard cores of the orthodox and Marxist economics research programmes. Nor does it attempt to enumerate the different weights which various groups of orthodox and Marxist economists would give to each aspect of these hard cores. Rather, it attempts to identify the major non-vague features of these hard cores and to highlight their distinctive differences by contrast with one another. Also, it should be noted that since the orthodox and Marxist research programmes are both long-standing programmes in economics, this contrast does not fall foul of the difficulty of distinguishing between '*ex ante* and *ex post* hard core propositions' (see Cross [1982a], p.331).

8.5 THE POSITIVE HEURISTIC OF THE MARXIST RESEARCH PROGRAMME

The distinctive differences, between the hard core of the Marxist research programme and the hard core of the orthodox research programme, indicate how Marx's economic analysis of mature capitalism stresses the explanatory roles of the forces and relations of production which characterize this specific stage of historical development. Hence the positive heuristic of the Marxist research programme may be expressed generally as: 'explain how the historically specific set of productive forces and social relations of production, associated with the capitalist mode of production, determines various economic phenomena such as exchange ratios between goods, the distribution of total income between different classes, and the process of economic development'.

Note, however, that whenever the positive heuristic of the Marxist research programme provides a set of suggestions, as to how the hard core of the programme is to be supplemented in order to provide an explanation of the various aspects of mature capitalism, these suggestions must ensure that the resulting analytical techniques, economic concepts and theories embody the essential features of the hard core hypotheses.

Thus, for example, since Marx's economic analysis of capitalism stresses the historically specific set of social relationships between economic agents which characterizes mature capitalism, then the positive heuristic of the Marxist research programme will require that each Marxist economic concept relates to this particular set of social or class relationships. In other words, the positive heuristic directs that the economic concepts of the Marxist research programme embody both a specific social and historical dimension.

The multi-dimensional character of analytical techniques and economic concepts

To enhance our understanding of the preceding paragraph, we shall now provide a few brief illustrations of how analytical techniques and economic concepts embody a multi-dimensional character in Marxist economic analysis.

As a first example, note that although Marxist economic analysis includes equilibrium analysis and the method of comparative statics, these analytical techniques are applied in a way that always emphasizes the underlying historically specific set of social relationships. Hence, in Marx's use of these techniques, the specific structure, and changes in this structure, of social relationships is of particular importance. In contrast, the equilibrium analysis and comparative statics of the orthodox research programme does not have this sociological dimension. Moreover, while an equilibrium in orthodox economics is a position which is characterized by a balance of forces, and hence is a situation in which there is no tendency for change, the Marxist dialectical analysis emphasizes the hidden tensions or contradictions (essentially resulting from the underlying class struggle) within apparently static situations, which operate as a driving force leading to the emergence of a new situation.

As a second example, note that, in common with the orthodox research programme, the Marxist analysis commences with simplifying assumptions which, as the research programme develops, are subsequently replaced by more sophisticated and more realistic assumptions. However, while (in our view) the orthodox economics approach is to move from, for example, unrealistic idealizations of market exchange towards a better explanation of the reality of market exchange, the Marxist economics approach is very different.

Thus, in the Marxist analysis, the approach is to start with the 'reality' of social relationships which lie beneath the 'appearance' of market exchange and then, by successively more sophisticated logical analysis of the social relationships, to approximate increasingly the 'appearance' in terms of the 'reality', so as to move towards a better explanation of what the 'appearance' actually is. Moreover, the *logical stages* in this process of successive approximation correspond to specific *historical stages* in the development of capitalism. Hence Marxist analysis explicitly uses what is known as a 'logical-historical method'. In addition, this integration of the logical analysis and historical development of capitalism is dialectical in character, with the contradictions inherent in one stage leading to the emergence of the next stage.

As a further example, note that the economic concept of 'capital', in the Marxist analysis, is not viewed simply as a 'thing' (namely, the physical means of production). Rather, capital is viewed as a particular social production relation which, in turn, is associated with a particular historical stage of development of society. Thus, in contrast to the concept of capital in orthodox economics, in the Marxist analysis the concept of capital explicitly includes both a social and a historical dimension.

In addition, while both Marxist and orthodox economics attempt to explain capital accumulation, the Marxist analysis contains a specific social and historical dimension whereas the orthodox analysis is asocial and ahistorical in character. Thus, in the Marxist analysis, the motivation of the capitalist, lying behind the Marxist assumption of a strong drive to accumulate capital, is analysed as arising out of the process of historical development prior to mature capitalism, and as such, is linked to a specific social form of production. Moreover, in the Marxist analysis, individual capitalists are viewed as being compelled to accumulate capital (independent of their subjective preferences), with this compulsion on individual capitalists operating via the mechanism of competition. In contrast, orthodox economics analyses capital accumulation in terms of a general economic motivation of individuals to maximize wealth, and to achieve a preferred time-pattern of consumption, subject to certain constraints which embody no specific social or historical dimension.

As a final example of the multi-dimensional character of analytical techniques and economic concepts in Marxist analysis, note that while Marx, in common with many areas of orthodox analysis, assumed free competition between capitalists, the social and historical dimension enters once more in the sense that his analysis of competition also stresses the social relation of capitalist to capitalist, and of capitalists to workers, within a specific historical context.

The Marxist research programme and its subprogrammes

Now that we have outlined both the hard core and the positive heuristic of the Marxist research programme, we can briefly note that the Marxist research programme (like the orthodox research programme) contains various subprogrammes. Thus, while there are considerably fewer economists working within the Marxist research programme (and hence subprogrammes are correspondingly less developed than many orthodox subprogrammes), various subprogrammes can be identified.

For example, one post-Marx development of the labour theory of value has given rise to a subprogramme concerned with explaining not only whether a coherent theory of relative prices can be derived from the labour theory of value, but also whether such a theory of prices can only be derived from the labour theory of value. Similarly, another development of the labour theory of value has given rise to a further subprogramme concerned with explaining how skilled labour can be reduced to unskilled labour.

Other subprogrammes are, for example, concerned with explaining the impact and effects of the class struggle in the workplace, with providing a Marxist explanation of state influence on the capitalist economy, and with providing a Marxist explanation of how the geographical expansion of capitalism (known as *capitalist imperialism*) affects both capitalist and non-capitalist economies.

Finally, note that each of the above-mentioned subprogrammes involves a specific application of the general positive heuristic, of the Marxist research programme, to the respective problem-situations listed in the two preceding paragraphs. Also, note that each of the subprogrammes *implies* the hard core of the Marxist research programme. This, in turn, means that (analogous to the appraisal of a subprogramme within the orthodox research programme) each subprogramme of the Marxist research programme can be appraised via the MSRP appraisal criteria of progressiveness and heuristic strength. In addition, analogous to the comparison of rival subprogrammes within the orthodox research programme, rival subprogrammes within the Marxist research programme can also be compared via the MSRP appraisal criteria.

Now that we have briefly outlined both the orthodox research programme and the Marxist research programme, and indicated some of their respective subprogrammes, we can proceed to a further examination of the difficulties which arise when we come to compare either the orthodox and Marxist research programmes or an orthodox subprogramme with a Marxist subprogramme. (For further discussion of Marxist analysis, and reference to Marxist subprogrammes, see Blaug [1980b], Bottomore [1983], Fine and Harris [1979], and Howard and King [1985].)

8.6 METAPHYSICS AND THE HARD CORE OF A RESEARCH PROGRAMME

The foregoing discussion has indicated that the orthodox and Marxist research programmes have very different, distinctive hard cores. In addition, the preceding discussion has indicated that the subprogrammes contained within each of these research programmes also imply the distinctive hard core of the respective, 'parent' research programme.

Now that we have seen this, we are in a position to note (following Koertge [1979a], p. 20) that each distinctive hard core represents a distinctive, conjectural *world picture* (or *metaphysics*). In other words, since the statements (or basic assumptions or hypotheses) contained in each distinctive hard core make claims or assertions about the fundamental nature of the economic situation (or domain) under investigation, these statements (known as *metaphysical statements*) provide what is known as a conjectural or speculative world picture. Thus, the unfalsifiable, distinctive hard core of a Lakatosian research programme can be viewed as providing an unfalsifiable, conjectural world picture. This means we can now speak of the hard core of the orthodox research programme as providing one conjectural world picture and the hard core of the Marxist research programme as providing another, very different, conjectural world picture.

Once we have noted that the hard core of a research programme provides a distinctive, conjectural world picture (or metaphysics), we can then proceed to note what *influence* this metaphysics has on theory construction within the research programme.

To do this, recall that the positive heuristic of a research programme provides a set of suggestions as to how the hard core of the programme is to be supplemented, in order for the programme to be capable of providing explanations and predictions of the phenomena under consideration. Hence, as such, the positive heuristic guides the production of specific theories within the programme, with each specific theory not only being 'constructed around' the programme's hard core (or conjectural world picture) but also implying that hard core (or conjectural world picture). In other words, the distinctive world picture underlying a research programme will have an influence on theory construction within the research programme, in the sense that each specific theory will not only be *constructed around* but will also *imply* the fundamental set of statements constituting this distinctive world picture.

To appreciate further how the specific metaphysics (or conjectural world picture) can influence theory construction, note that the specific metaphysics does not provide *detailed* guidance about the exact form that any theory should take. While this is so, note however that the positive heuristic of the research programme must ensure that the resulting analytical techniques, economic concepts and theories embody the essential features of the hard core hypotheses (or specific metaphysics) underlying the research programme.

Thus, for example, in the earlier discussion of the Marxist research programme, we saw that since Marx's economic analysis of capitalism is derived from the historically specific set of social relationships, between economic agents, which characterize mature capitalism, then the positive heuristic of the Marxist research programme will require that each Marxist economic concept relates to this particular set of social or class relationships. In other words, the positive heuristic directs that the economic concepts of the Marxist research programme embody both a specific social and historical dimension. In contrast, the positive heuristic of the orthodox research programme (in keeping with the hard core hypotheses or specific metaphysics of the orthodox research programme) does not require the resulting analytical techniques, economic concepts and theories to embody such a social and historical dimension.

The important point to note, from the preceding four paragraphs, is that the specific metaphysics underlying a research programme has an important *regulative influence* on theory construction within the research programme. In other words, the specific metaphysics regulates the construction of theories by suggesting a certain range of theoretical possibilities. This, in turn, implies that the specific metaphysics explicitly rules out a range of other theoretical possibilities. The discussion, in Sections 8.4 and 8.5, of the hard core and positive heuristic of the Marxist research programme, and their contrast to the hard core and positive heuristic of the orthodox research programme, should suffice to illustrate how a specific metaphysics exerts an important and distinctive regulative influence on theory construction (and hence on economic analysis) within a research programme.

Metaphysics and commitment

The above discussion has indicated that the hard core of a research programme provides a distinctive, conjectural world picture (or metaphysics). While it is important to recognize this, it is also important to recognize that this does *not* mean that every economics researcher, working within a given research programme, views the programme's hard core either as the true representation of the world or as representing how the world should be viewed.

Also, while the above discussion has indicated how the specific metaphysics underlying a research programme exerts an important regulative influence on theory construction (and hence on economic analysis) within that research programme, this does *not* mean that every economics researcher working within the research programme believes that all theory construction (and hence all economic analysis) should be based on this specific metaphysics exclusively.

Finally, while the specific metaphysics underlying a research programme does influence theory construction (and hence economic analysis) within that research programme, this does *not* mean that every economics researcher working within that research programme believes that all economic policy recommendations should be based exclusively on the theoretical predictions of the theories, and economic analysis, which have been generated under the influence of this specific metaphysics.

It may well be that some economics researchers, working within a given research programme, *are* personally committed to the specific metaphysics underlying that research programme. Thus, it may well be that some economics researchers believe (for example, on ethical, social or political grounds) not only that this specific metaphysics is a true representation of the world but also that it should influence all theory construction, economic analysis, and policy recommendations. However, it is important to recognize that economics researchers, working within a given research programme, are *not* automatically, and necessarily, personally committed to the specific metaphysics underlying that research programme. Rather, it is possible to work within a given research programme without believing that its specific metaphysics constitutes the basic structure which should underlie all theory construction, economic analysis and policy recommendations.

8.7 POSITIVE AND NORMATIVE STATEMENTS

Now that we have claimed that it is possible for economics researchers to work within a research programme (and engage in theory construction, economic analysis and economic policy recommendations) without *necessarily* having a personal commitment to that programme's metaphysics, we shall proceed to substantiate this claim.

Explanation, prediction and commitment

To do this, note that the following *conditional statement* need not involve personal commitment to a research programme's specific metaphysics: '*if* a research programme's specific metaphysics is given by a set of statements A, and *if* the set of theories constructed around this specific metaphysics is given by the set B, and *if* the initial conditions (which provide details of the particular economic situation under investigation) are given by the set C, *then* logical deduction (or theoretical analysis) indicates that the set of theoretical predictions (or consequences) is given by the set D'. Consequently, if economics researchers' work within a given research programme proceeds in terms of such conditional (or *if-then*) statements, then this means that their research work need not involve personal commitment to the research programme's specific metaphysics.

In order to enhance our understanding of the preceding paragraph, let us assume that economics researchers are using the orthodox research programme as a basis for investigating some economic situation. Having made this assumption, note that the hard core of the orthodox research programme makes specific assertions (or conjectures) about the fundamental nature of the economic situation under investigation.

Thus, for example, the hard core (or conjectural world picture) of the orthodox research programme asserts (in contrast to the hard core of the conjectural world picture of the Marxist research programme) individualism rather than the social nature of the individual economic agent, rational behaviour of individual economic agents rather than rationality with a social dimension, property ownership as ownership of 'things' rather than as a social power relation, and market exchange as a relationship between 'things' rather than a simultaneous relationship between 'things' and between people.

In addition, note that since the above economics researchers are basing their economic analysis on the 'orthodox' hard core, then the specific theories which will be subsequently constructed (in an attempt to explain the phenomena under consideration), will not only be 'constructed around' but will also *imply* this 'orthodox' hard core (or conjectural world picture). This, in turn, means that the theoretical predictions which will be generated will also *imply* the 'orthodox' hard core. In other words, the whole investigation is essentially concerned with providing an 'orthodox' explanation of the phenomena under consideration.

Having made this observation, note immediately that if we had alternatively assumed that the above economics researchers are using the Marxist research programme as a basis for investigating economic situations, then the theories would instead not only be 'constructed around' but would also *imply* the 'Marxist' hard core (or conjectural world picture), with its assertions about the social nature of individual economic agents, rationality with a social dimension, property ownership as a social power relation, market exchange as a simultaneous relationship between 'things' and between people, the materialist conception of history, and dialectical historical change. This, in turn, would mean that the generated theoretical predictions would then also *imply* the 'Marxist' hard core. Hence, given this alternative assumption, the whole investigation would instead be concerned with providing a 'Marxist' explanation of the phenomena under consideration.

Note, however, that it is possible for economics researchers to provide, say, an 'orthodox' explanation of certain phenomena without *necessarily* being personally committed to the 'orthodox' world picture. In other words, it is quite possible for economics researchers, working within the orthodox research programme, to generate theoretical predictions and then test them, without necessarily being personally committed to the 'orthodox' world picture. (Note, in keeping with Section 7.5, that if some theories take the form of untestable idealizations, then some of the theoretical predictions may also be untestable.)

Hence, it is by no means unusual for economics researchers to provide such an 'orthodox' explanation, and then subject it to empirical testing, without necessarily believing that the world picture contained in the 'orthodox' hard core is correct (or more correct than, say, the world picture contained in the Marxist research programme).

Moreover, economics researchers can provide such an 'orthodox' explanation in the full awareness that this 'orthodox' explanation has excluded other theoretical possibilities (such as those contained in a 'Marxist' explanation), without necessarily believing that only 'orthodox' explanations of economic phenomena should be considered. Consequently, it should be clear that it is quite possible for economics researchers to present such an 'orthodox' explanation as an *objective*, *declarative* statement of the predictions which can be logically deduced from 'orthodox' premises (and subsequently exposed to empirical testing), rather than as a *subjective*, *evaluative* statement of how they believe the given economic situation should be viewed.

Economic policy recommendations and commitment

In a similar fashion, economics researchers, working within a given research programme, can present economic policy recommendations in the form of objective, declarative statements without *necessarily* being personally committed to that programme's specific metaphysics (or conjectural world picture). For example, the following conditional statement need not involve personal commitment to a research programme's specific metaphysics: '*if* the theories, which have not only been constructed around but also imply the specific metaphysics of a given research programme, are taken as a basis for making economic policy recommendations, and *if* a particular objective (for example, such as a reduction in unemployment) is assumed, *then* logical deduction (or theoretical analysis) indicates that such and such policy measures should be undertaken'.

In other words, if we take a given research programme as a basis for economic policy recommendations, then we can deduce what policy measures should be undertaken in order to achieve a given policy objective, without necessarily being personally committed *either* to the given research programme's specific metaphysics *or* to the given objective.

To reinforce the argument of the preceding two paragraphs, let us note exactly what the preceding conditional statement does *not* say. Firstly, note that it does *not* say that the research programme's specific metaphysics (or world picture) should actually be accepted. Secondly, note that it does *not* say that the given objective should actually be accepted. Lastly, note that it does *not* say that the recommended policy measures should actually be put into operation.

In other words, the conditional statement, given in the first paragraph of this sub-section, is *not* concerned with the *ethical desirability* of (a) the research programme's specific metaphysics, (b) the given objective, or (c) the deduced policy measures. Rather, it is merely concerned with the *logical deductibility* of particular conclusions (the policy recommendations) from certain premises or assumptions (the theories based on the research programme's specific metaphysics and the given objective). Hence, rather than the preceding conditional statement necessarily representing the economics researchers' *prescriptive evaluation* of some economic situation, it is simply an *objective*, *declarative* statement of the policy recommendations that can be logically deduced from certain premises (see also Ng [1972] and [1983], Chapter 1).

The distinction between positive and normative statements

By this stage, it should be clear that the above discussion has made an important distinction between *objective*, *declarative* statements about an economic situation and *prescriptive evaluations* of that economic situation. As a matter of terminology, let us now note that the former statements are known as *positive statements*, whereas the latter are known as *normative statements*. Also, let us note that positive statements are essentially concerned with what *is*, whereas normative statements are essentially concerned with what *ought* to be.

Thus, as we have seen, *positive statements* are objective, declarative statements which are not only concerned with what is being asserted (or conjectured) about an economic situation, but also with the logical conclusions of certain premises. In contrast, *normative statements* are concerned with prescriptive evaluations of an economic situation, with how this situation ought to be analysed, with what is morally right or wrong, good or bad, in relation to this situation (see Ng [1983], Chapter 1).

Consequently, given this terminology, if an economics researcher, working within a given research programme, presents his analysis in terms of positive statements, then this means that his work need not involve personal commitment to the programme's specific metaphysics (or world picture). Moreover, note that the theoretical predictions of his analysis can be falsified by empirical tests (except in the case where the theories take the form of untestable idealizations which give rise to deduced predictions which are also untestable).

On the other hand, if an economics researcher, working within a given research programme, deliberately presents his whole analysis in terms of normative statements, then this means that his work necessarily involves personal commitment to the programme's specific metaphysics. Also, in the latter case, note that while the normative statements can be criticized and debated, they cannot be empirically tested and falsified in the same way as positive statements (as can be readily seen, for example, by comparing the positive statement that 'the total quantity of good x demanded per week, in the given market, is inversely related to the price per unit of good x', with the normative statement that 'good x ought to be supplied free of charge to everyone over 60 years of age').

8.8 DIFFICULTIES IN THE COMPARISON OF RIVAL RESEARCH PROGRAMMES

In Section 8.6, we noted that the hard core of a research programme provides a distinctive, conjectural world picture (or metaphysics). Also, in Section 8.7, we noted that it is possible for economics researchers to work within a research programme (and engage in theory construction, economic analysis and economic policy recommendations) without necessarily having a personal commitment to the programme's metaphysics. Now that we have clarified these points, we shall proceed to examine some of the difficulties which arise in the comparison of rival research programmes. In doing so, note that we shall initially assume that each of the economics researchers, working within a given research programme, does *not* have a personal commitment to that programme's specific metaphysics. Also, note that while our comments will initially refer to the comparison of *research programmes*, we shall subsequently refer to the comparison of *subprogrammes*.

As noted in Section 8.1, the relative merits of competing research programmes are to be evaluated, according to MSRP, by reference to their respective degrees of explanatory power or progressiveness. Thus, in such comparisons, if one research programme is capable not only of explaining the previous successes of a rival programme, but also of providing additional novel explanatory content which has been empirically confirmed, then MSRP appraises it as superior to its rival. Also, as noted in Section 8.1, the appraisal of competing research programmes is to include a comparison of each programme's heuristic strength. Hence, if one research programme is both more progressive and heuristically stronger than its rival, then MSRP appraises it as superior to its rival.

Abandoning a degenerate research programme in favour of its progressive rival

If we consider the situation where, over a period of time, one research programme has become increasingly progressive whereas its rival has become increasingly degenerative, then not only do the MSRP appraisal criteria declare the former research programme to be superior to the latter, but they also provide an objective reason for 'abandoning' the latter research programme. In other words, since the progressive research programme has not only explained the degenerate research programme's previous successes, but has also generated additional, empirically-confirmed, novel explanatory content, then this provides logical and empirical grounds for 'abandoning' the degenerate research programme in favour of its progressive rival. Hence, in such a situation, economics researchers working within the degenerate research programme have an objective reason for ceasing to work within this programme, and instead starting to work within the rival, progressive programme.

(The reason for the inverted commas around the word abandoning is that MSRP allows for the possibility that the degenerate research programme may make a comeback and subsequently become more progressive than its rival. Hence, MSRP recognizes that an economics researcher may continue to work within such a degenerate research programme, even though he accepts that it is currently inferior to its rival and even though he has no personal commitment to its specific metaphysics, in the hope that it can make a comeback and eventually supersede its rival.)

Since the progressive research programme has both explained the degenerate research programme's previous successes and generated additional, empirically-confirmed, novel explanatory content, then MSRP takes this as an indication that the theories produced by the progressive research programme *appear* to be a better approximation to the truth than the theories produced by the degenerate research programme. Hence, not only does MSRP view the body of economic knowledge as growing via the succession of progressive research programmes constantly superseding their degenerate rivals, but it also concludes that there is every indication that this growing body of knowledge is gradually improving its approximation to the truth.

Obviously it is hoped that the growing body of economic knowledge is not only gradually improving its *apparent* approximation to the truth, but also it is gradually improving its *actual* approximation to the truth. However, according to MSRP, there is no guarantee that this is so. Analogously to falsificationism, MSRP argues that there is no way of establishing that actual (rather than apparent) convergence towards the truth is taking place.

Hence, MSRP argues that the most we can claim is that there is every indication that the current body of economic knowledge is the best approximation to the truth. Note, however, that while this claim may be less than we would like to be able to claim, it does nonetheless provide an objective reason for basing explanations, predictions and policy recommendations on the theories produced by a progressive research programme rather than on the theories produced by its degenerate rival. (Also note that the foregoing theoretical predictions and policy recommendations are assumed to be in the form of *positive* statements.)

How is the hard core of a superseding research programme to be viewed?

In the preceding sub-section we noted how, in the situation of a progressive research programme superseding its degenerate rival, MSRP provides an objective reason for 'abandoning' the degenerate research programme in favour of its progressive rival. Having noted this, also note that if the degenerate research programme is 'abandoned', then this in turn means that the degenerate research programme's hard core (and agenda for generating changes in the programme's protective belt) will also be 'abandoned'. (Note, however, that this does *not* mean that the hard core of the degenerate research programme is falsified. This follows from the fact that the hard core of a Lakatosian research programme is deemed unfalsifiable throughout.)

Now that the hard core of the degenerate research programme has been 'abandoned', we can proceed to consider how the hard core of its progressive, superseding rival is to be viewed.

To do this, let us suppose that this superseding research programme has not only had a long progressive development, but has also demonstrated its considerable heuristic strength. Given this background, plus the fact that its rival has not only degenerated but has also been 'abandoned', does this mean that the hard core of the superseding research programme has become well 'corroborated' in some sense? In other words, has the specific metaphysics (or conjectural world picture), contained in the hard core of the superseding research programme, become well 'corroborated' in some sense, so as to enable us to conclude that this specific metaphysics *appears* to be a better approximation to the truth than the specific metaphysics of the degenerate research programme?

The answer to this question is no. To regard the hard core of the superseding research programme as well 'corroborated' (as does Watkins [1958]), because the theories built around (and implying) this hard core have been empirically confirmed by a large number of rigorous empirical tests, would be tantamount to allowing such empirical confirmations to count in favour of the hard core while, at the same time, not allowing anything to count against it (because the hard core is deemed irrefutable). Clearly this would be unsatisfactory (see Koertge [1979a], p. 29).

Moreover, it is important to recognize that successful (or empirically-confirmed) theories may be built around a hard core containing basic propositions or assumptions which are all false. (Recall, in our discussion of instrumentalism in Chapter 3, how empirically successful predictions may be logically deduced from an argument containing a false assumption.) Likewise, it is important to recognize that successful theories may also be built around a hard core containing basic propositions or assumptions which are either all true (even though they have not been proven to be true) or some are true and some are false.

A recognition of these points indicates that it is possible for the hard core of the superseding research programme to be a *poorer* approximation to the truth than the hard core of its degenerate, 'abandoned' rival. Consequently, it is unsatisfactory to regard the hard core of the superseding research programme as well 'corroborated' because the theories built around it are empirically successful.

But what about the situation where the empirically-confirmed theories of the superseding research programme *conflict* with the hard core (or specific metaphysics) of its degenerate, 'abandoned' rival? Does this mean that the hard core of the latter programme has been 'refuted' in some sense (as suggested by Wisdom [1963] and [1987a], Chapter 15) and, consequently, that the currently 'unrefuted' hard core of the superseding research programme should be regarded as a better approximation to the truth than the hard core of its rival?

The answer is no. If the superseding research programme does not provide an ultimate explanation of reality, then it is quite possible that a subsequent revival of the degenerate programme may result in its being regarded as progressive, and the former progressive research programme being regarded as degenerate. Hence, it is difficult to support the contention that the hard core of the degenerate research programme has been 'refuted' in some sense and, consequently, that the current 'unrefuted' hard core of the superseding research programme should be regarded as a better approximation to the truth than the hard core of its rival.

Note that, despite the difficulties associated with the above kind of scientific 'refutation' of metaphysics, it is nonetheless possible to take the view that whenever the well tested and empirically successful scientific theories of a research programme conflict with metaphysics, it is the metaphysics which should give way and be abandoned (for example, see Koertge [1979a], p. 28). However, while the above kind of scientific 'refutation' of metaphysics may have taken place in the 'natural sciences' (as Koertge claims, *loc. cit.*), it is extremely difficult to obtain such 'refutation' in the current state of economics (as we shall note in the next sub-section).

In the preceding sub-section we noted that since the superseding research programme has explained the degenerate, 'abandoned' research programme's previous successes and generated additional, empirically-confirmed, novel explanatory content, then MSRP takes this as an indication that the theories produced by the superseding research programme *appear* to be a better approximation to the truth than the theories produced by its degenerate, 'abandoned' rival. However, given the discussion in this sub-section, it should now be clear that we cannot infer from this that the specific metaphysics (or hard core) of the superseding research programme is well 'corroborated' in some sense, or that this specific metaphysics *appears* to be a better approximation to the truth than the specific metaphysics of the degenerate, 'abandoned' research programme. In addition, the above discussion has indicated that even though the empirically confirmed theories of the superseding research programme may conflict directly with the specific metaphysics (or hard core) of its degenerate, 'abandoned' rival, this does not enable us to infer that the specific metaphysics of the latter programme has been 'refuted' in some sense (though one may wish to take this conflict as grounds for abandoning the latter metaphysics).

Thus, while MSRP provides an objective reason for basing explanations, predictions and policy recommendations on the theories built around (and implying) the specific metaphysics (or hard core) of the superseding research programme, rather than on the theories built around (and implying) the specific metaphysics of its degenerate, 'abandoned' rival, we must be careful not to make erroneous inferences from this about the specific metaphysics of the superseding research programme. In particular, we cannot infer that the specific metaphysics of the superseding research programme is either well 'corroborated' in some sense or that it *appears* to be a better approximation to the truth than the specific metaphysics of its degenerate, 'abandoned' rival.

The difficulty of obtaining clear-cut supersession in economics

Now that we have clarified what is involved in a research programme superseding its rival, we can proceed to note how difficult it is to obtain clear-cut supersession in economics.

One immediate difficulty in assessing whether or not a research programme has superseded its rival arises from the possibility that a degenerate research programme may subsequently revive and reverse the assessment. In other words, MSRP does not provide us with appraisal criteria that enable us to make a clear-cut, once-for-all assessment of supersession. Moreover, even if we ignore this problem, it is by no means easy to assess that a given research programme has superseded its rival at a given point in time.

As noted in Section 8.1, it is very difficult to precisely appraise a research programme, at a given point in time, because such an appraisal generally involves appraising a mix of tested, untested (though testable) and untestable theories. Moreover, as noted in Section 7.6, even in the case of testable theories, economics researchers are still faced with the difficulty of obtaining conclusive empirical results from the empirical testing of theories in economics.

Finally, when we add to these difficulties the problems of comparing the content of research programmes (and our discussion of the orthodox and Marxist research programmes should suffice to indicate the extent to which economics research programmes can differ in content), and of assessing the relative heuristic power of research programmes, we can see that it is extremely difficult to assess whether or not a research programme has superseded its rival at a given point in time. This, in turn, helps to explain why two rival economics research programmes may co-exist for a considerable period of time, without one research programme clearly superseding its rival. Also, the above difficulties help to explain why the Wisdom-type of scientific 'refutation' of metaphysics is extremely difficult to obtain in the current state of economics.

It should be noted that the above difficulties, involved in comparing rival *research programmes*, are also involved in comparing rival *subprogrammes*, whether these rival subprogrammes are located within the same research programme or in different research programmes. However, while rival subprogrammes which are located within different research programmes may face considerable content-comparison problems, it is to be expected that rival subprogrammes within the same research programme would face lesser content-comparison problems. Hence, within a given research programme, it may be less difficult to assess whether or not a subprogramme has superseded its rival.

(The comments in the preceding paragraph remind us that the appraisal of a given research programme, at a point in time, involves the appraisal of a set of subprogrammes. Since the subprogrammes of a given research programme may be at different stages of progressiveness and/or degeneracy, this further complicates the assessment of whether or not a research programme has superseded its rival.)

It should also be noted that, in the case (within a given research programme) where a progressive subprogramme supersedes a degenerate, 'abandoned' rival subprogramme, both subprogrammes will still continue to imply the hard core (or specific metaphysics) of the 'parent' research programme to which they both belong. In addition, whereas the distinctive positive heuristic guidelines relating to the 'abandoned', superseded subprogramme may be abandoned, the general positive heuristic of the 'parent' research programme will be unaffected by this supersession.

Now that we have noted the difficulty of obtaining clear-cut supersession in economics, we shall proceed to note briefly how this in turn gives rise to difficulties in the comparison of rival policy recommendations.

8.9 DIFFICULTIES IN THE COMPARISON OF RIVAL POLICY RECOMMENDATIONS

The above discussion implies that if we had a clear-cut case of a progressive research programme (or subprogramme) superseding its degenerate, 'abandoned' rival, then (according to MSRP) this would provide an objective reason for basing explanations, predictions, and policy recommendations on the theories produced by the progressive superseding research programme (or subprogramme), rather than on the theories produced by its degenerate rival.

Hence, if we continue to assume that each of the economics researchers, working within a given research programme, does not have a personal commitment to that programme's specific metaphysics (or world picture), then such clear-cut supersession (with no content-comparison problems, etc.), means that the theories of the superseding research programme (or subprogramme) can be used to provide theoretical predictions and policy recommendations (in the form of positive statements).

Unfortunately, as noted in the preceding sub-section, such clear-cut supersession is not readily forthcoming in the current state of economics, except perhaps in the case of fairly commensurable subprogrammes within a given research programme. This lack of clear-cut supersession does not, however, mean that policy recommendations cannot be made. Rather it means that, in order to avoid confusion in policy comparisons, policy recommendations need to be accompanied by statements which clarify exactly what such policy recommendations are based on.

Policy recommendations often include subjective judgements
In order to clarify what we mean by the last sentence of the preceding paragraph, let us suppose that rival policy recommendations have been produced by economics researchers working on two competing *subprogrammes* which, in turn, belong to the same 'parent' research programme. Also, let us suppose that the respective policy recommendations are accompanied by statements of the assumptions on which they are based, plus statements of the extent to which the theories underlying the policy recommendations have been confirmed by empirical tests.

Having made these assumptions, let us also make the important observation that such policy recommendations will often include certain *subjective judgements*. In other words, given the economics researchers' imperfect knowledge, not only about how the relevant economic situation is currently structured but also about how the respective policy measures would affect this economic situation if implemented, the economic researchers may make *subjective judgements* about these imperfectly understood matters, and incorporate these subjective judgements within their respective policy recommendations (see Ng [1972] and [1983], Appendix 1A).

(Note that the policy recommendations can still be presented in terms of positive statements of the form: 'if such and such assumptions are made, and if such and such subjective judgements are also made, then such and such policy recommendations can be deduced from these assumptions and subjective judgements'.)

Having made the important observation that the rival policy recommendations, produced by economics researchers working on two competing subprogrammes within a given research programme, will often include various subjective judgements, note that this helps to explain why there may be considerable disagreement among economics researchers over such policy recommendations (even though there may be no disagreement among these economics researchers over the specific metaphysics contained in the 'parent' research programme's hard core).

Further sources of disagreement over policy matters

If we now move to the situation where two competing *research programmes* coexist, then it is likely that there will be even more disagreement among economics researchers over policy matters. Clearly, when we consider the distinctive, very different hard cores and positive heuristics of the orthodox and Marxist research programmes, it is not surprising that we find conflicting policy recommendations based on 'orthodox' and 'Marxist' theories. For example, while orthodox policy recommendations in response to (say) the problems of unemployment and inflation may involve various monetary and fiscal strategies, these strategies are such that they explicitly assume that the prevailing system of capitalism will continue to exist. In sharp contrast, the only Marxist policy recommendation that can be regarded as an ultimately adequate response, to these same problems, would explicitly require a complete change in the structure of ownership of the means of production and the demise of capitalism.

When we also take into account the various subjective judgements included in these very different policy recommendations (for example, with respect to the specific details, magnitude, and timing of the changes entailed by these recommendations), then it is not surprising that such a situation gives rise to considerable disagreement over policy matters. (For further discussion of orthodox and Marxist macroeconomic policy recommendations, see Dow [1985], Chapter 8.)

To add to the complexity of the preceding situation, it should be noted that the possible sources for disagreement over policy matters will be increased when the economics researchers, working within a particular research programme, have a personal commitment to the specific metaphysics (or conjectural world picture) contained in the hard core of that research programme.

Thus, for example, an economics researcher with a personal commitment to the specific metaphysics contained in the hard core of the Marxist research programme, may continue to support policy recommendations based on 'Marxist' theories even though he may currently view the orthodox research programme as more progressive (on MSRP criteria) than the Marxist research programme. His reason for doing this may be simply that, given his personal commitment to the Marxist world picture, he views the policy recommendations produced by the Marxist research programme as a 'progressive' *political action programme* and the policy recommendations produced by the orthodox research programme as a 'degenerate' political action programme (with this terminology taken from Blaug [1980a], p. 260).

However, while this additional complication may exist, it is important to note that this need *not* hinder the objective, positive analysis of the policy recommendations of competing research programmes. In other words, it is quite possible for economics researchers to present the respective policy recommendations in the form of positive statements and then, separately, add normative statements containing their personal views as to which policy recommendations should be implemented.

It is also important to note that the adoption of MSRP in economics would help to clarify such complex situations. Essentially it would do this by stressing that the theories (and hence the theoretical predictions and policy recommendations) produced by a given research programme are built around and imply the specific metaphysics (or world picture) contained in that research programme's hard core. In other words, once this link between policy recommendations and a specific metaphysics (or world picture) is made explicit, then it is much easier to see why economics researchers with personal commitments to different world pictures will disagree over policy matters.

It is our opinion that this important clarification, provided by an awareness of the specific metaphysics underlying theoretical predictions and policy recommendations, provides an important reason for retaining the hard core/protective belt distinction within a research programme (and, therefore, an important reason for rejecting Cross's view, in Cross [1982a], that it is better to drop this distinction).

Before leaving this sub-section, note that disagreement over policy matters, resulting from economics researchers' personal commitment to different political action programmes, can also arise in relation to the rival policy recommendations of competing subprogrammes belonging to the same 'parent' research programme. Thus, for example, disagreement may arise in a situation where economics researchers working within one orthodox macroeconomics subprogramme recommend more government intervention in the economy, whereas economics researchers working within another orthodox macroeconomics subprogramme recommend less government intervention in the economy. In other words, both sets of economics researchers may accept the specific metaphysics contained in the hard core of the orthodox research programme, yet still disagree over the extent of government intervention in the economy.

Moreover, to complicate matters further, note that while part of this disagreement may be due to personal commitment to different, wider world pictures defined as containing both the hard core of the orthodox research programme and additional ethical, social and political elements, part may also be due to different subjective judgements (about how the relevant economic situation is currently structured and about how the respective policy recommendations would affect this economic situation if implemented), which are quite independent of the economics researchers' personal commitments to particular world pictures.

Once more, however, these complications need *not* hinder the objective, positive analysis of the policy recommendations of competing subprogrammes. In other words, the respective policy recommendations can still be presented in terms of positive statements, accompanied by statements indicating the relevant subjective judgements and/or statements indicating personal views about which policy recommendations should be implemented.

Basic and non-basic value judgements

In the preceding sub-sections, we have noted that economics researchers may have personal commitments to different world pictures (or specific metaphysics). In other words, economics researchers may have different *value judgements* about how the domain (or economic situation) under investigation should be structured. As hinted above, these value judgements may extend considerably beyond the hard core statements of a particular research programme to incorporate judgements not only about what ought to be, but also about what is morally right or wrong, and good or bad, with regard to ethical, social, religious and political considerations.

Note, however, that while economics researchers may have different value judgements, including different value judgements about the specific metaphysics (or hard core) that should underlie economics analysis and policy recommendations, this does *not* mean that these different value judgements cannot be discussed or criticized.

For example, let us suppose that one group of economics researchers holds the value judgement that the hard core (or specific metaphysics) of the orthodox research programme should underlie the economic analysis of capitalist economies, whereas another group of economics researchers holds the value judgement that the hard core (or specific metaphysics) of the Marxist research programme should underlie the economic analysis of capitalist economies. Given this situation, note immediately that rational debate about these value judgements is quite possible. Moreover, note that such debate need not be confined solely to exercises in ethical, social and political persuasion (by which one group tries to persuade the other group to change its value judgements). In particular, it should be noted that positive analysis can also make an important contribution to such debates.

One very important contribution, that such positive analysis can make, is to point out the implications which can be logically deduced from the premises given by a particular set of value judgements. In other words, such positive analysis takes the form: 'if certain value judgements are taken as the premises underlying economic analysis, and if certain objectives are given, then the following implications can be logically deduced'. Since the logical implications of value judgements are often far from obvious, and since logical inconsistencies between value judgements (held by the same person) are also often far from obvious, positive analysis can provide important information about both what value judgements imply and possible inconsistencies between value judgements (see Sugden [1981], Chapter 1).

In addition, positive analysis can also introduce important empirical information into the debate over value judgements. For example, such positive analysis may take the form: 'if certain value judgements (or a certain specific metaphysics or a certain hard core) are taken as the premises underlying economic analysis, and if a certain positive heuristic is used, then the following theoretical predictions can be deduced and subsequently exposed to empirical testing'. Thus, as the results of such empirical testing become available, economics researchers will be provided with important information about whether or not the theoretical predictions, based on and implying the given hard core (or value judgements), are empirically confirmed.

Not only does the (logical and empirical) positive analysis introduce additional, important information into the debate over value judgements, but it may also *influence* these value judgements. In other words, the additional information provided by the positive analysis may lead certain economics researchers to change their value judgements.

Note, as a matter of terminology, that value judgements which may be influenced or changed as a result of ethical, social or political persuasion, and/or positive analysis, are known as *non-basic* value judgements. Alternatively, if value judgements are not open to influence or change, but are regarded by the holders as applicable under all conceivable conditions, they are known as *basic* value judgements (see Sen [1967] and [1970], Chapter 5).

Having introduced this terminology, it is important to note that rational debate about basic value judgements is quite possible, whether in the form of ethical, social or political persuasion or in the form of (logical and empirical) positive analysis. Essentially it is such debate that clarifies whether claimed basic value judgements are indeed truly basic rather than non-basic. In other words, if such debate fails to influence a set of basic value judgements, then such value judgements can be regarded as basic. Contrariwise, if such debate succeeds in influencing value judgements that were previously regarded as basic, then these value judgements must now be viewed as non-basic rather than basic. Also, it should be noted that MSRP aids this process of clarification, by making explicit the specific metaphysics underlying the theoretical predictions and policy recommendations produced by a given research programme.

Finally, note that if certain economics researchers hold the *basic* value judgement that the specific metaphysics contained in the hard core of a particular research programme, should underlie *all* economic analysis and policy recommendations, then this will affect their appraisal of the economic analysis and policy recommendations produced by rival research programmes. Consequently, even though they may recognize that a rival research programme may be appraised as progressive on the basis of MSRP appraisal criteria, they will still regard its analysis as a completely inadequate explanation of the economic situation under investigation. In addition, they may feel that the hard core (or world picture) of a rival research programme is so objectionable, on ethical, social and political grounds, that they would not work within such a rival research programme, except perhaps in order to criticize it and point out its inadequacies.

The complexity of comparing rival policy recommendations

The above discussion clearly indicates that the comparison of the rival policy recommendations of competing research programmes is a very complex matter. Not only do we have the difficulty of obtaining clear-cut supersession of research programmes in economics, but we also have the problem of comparing different basic and non-basic value judgements. Since the latter problem raises difficult questions not only about how such comparison should be made, but also about whether or not there is a set of value judgements (or a world picture) which is absolutely and uniquely correct, it should be evident just how complex the comparison of rival policy recommendations really is.

Moreover, to complicate matters even further, note that the discussion of the relative merits of rival policy recommendations generally takes place against a background of currently-implemented economic policies which, in turn, are often based on policy recommendations produced by *more than one* research programme.

However, while this complexity exists, the above discussion has indicated that there is still plenty of scope for (logical and empirical) positive analysis in economics. Also, it has indicated that while MSRP faces severe limitations when it comes to comparing rival research programmes and rival policy recommendations, it does nonetheless have important pedagogic value in the sense that its adoption helps to identify where many of the complications are located.

Before ending this chapter with a brief summary, note that Chapter 9 contains a discussion outlining not only the extent to which Lakatos's methodology was influenced by the methodological work of Thomas S. Kuhn, but also the important differences between the methodological viewpoints of Kuhn and Lakatos. In addition, note that Chapter 11 (which contains concluding comments) also contains further general comments about the implications of adopting MSRP in economics.

8.10 SUMMARY

In Chapter 7 we noted how difficult it is to appraise precisely a research programme at a given point in time, due not only to its mix of tested, untested (though testable) and untestable theories, but also to the problem of obtaining conclusive empirical results from the empirical testing of theories in economics. This difficulty, in turn, leads to difficulties in the appraisal of competing research programmes.

To make matters even more complicated, the appraisal of competing research programmes is faced with the fact that rival research programmes are often very different in content. Thus, as illustrated (in Sections 8.2-8.6) by reference to the orthodox and Marxist research programmes, and their respective subprogrammes, this chapter has shown that these differences in content arise from the fact that each of the rival research programmes has both a distinctive hard core (or specific metaphysics or world picture) and a distinctive positive heuristic underlying its economic analysis and policy recommendations. As noted in Sections 8.6-8.9, while these differences in content make the comparison of rival research programmes and rival policy recommendations exceedingly complex, there is still considerable scope (and an important need) for positive analysis in economics.

Finally, while the adoption of MSRP in economics does not provide a comprehensive solution to the complex problem of the comparison of rival research programmes and rival policy recommendations (and, given the complexity of such comparison, it is somewhat unrealistic to expect a methodology to do so), it does provide important insights into where many of the complications are located.

References for further reading

For further discussion and applications of MSRP to economics, see Archibald [1979]; Blaug [1976], [1980a] and [1980b]; Cross [1982a] and [1982b]; De Marchi [1976]; Fisher [1986]; Hands [1984] and [1985b]; Hutchison [1976] and [1981a]; Latsis [[1976]; Leijonhufvud [1976]; O'Brien [1983]; Remenyi [1979]; Rizzo [1982]; Schmidt [1982]; and Weintraub [1979] and [1985].

Additional details of Marxist analysis can be found in Aaronovitch and Smith [1981]; Blaug [1980b]; Bottomore [1983]; Dow [1985]; Fine [1980] and [1984]; Fine and Harris [1979]; Howard and King [1985]; Hunt [1979], Chapters 9, 10 and 19; Junankar [1982]; and Marx [1970] and [1973].

For further discussion of metaphysics and its relation to the hard core of a Lakatosian research programme, see Agassi [1964] and [1975]; Glass and Johnson [1988]; Koertge [1979a], [1979b] and [1981]; Popper [1972d], Chapter 8; Watkins [1958] and [1975]; and Wisdom [1963] and [1987], Chapter 15.

In addition to the references given in Sections 8.7-8.9, students will find Klappholz [1964] and Hutchison [1964] helpful.

9 Kuhn's Normal Science and Revolutionary Science

At the beginning of Chapter 5, we noted that descriptions of how economics researchers have actually proceeded in practice are often very different from the falsificationist account of how they should proceed in order to promote the growth of economic knowledge. Not only have economists continued to use theories which have been born refuted but they have also tenaciously held on to certain theories, for some time period, even after they were well aware of evidence which falsified or refuted these theories. In addition, economics research has often been characterized by numerous theoretical developments which are accompanied by both a relatively small amount of empirical testing and a relatively low regard for empirical refutations. To the extent that there is an important rationale for this non-falsificationist behaviour, then such behaviour can be taken as grounds for criticizing falsificationism as inadequate.

In Chapters 5-8 we examined how Lakatos's methodology of scientific research programmes (MSRP) attempts to improve upon falsificationism and provide an explanation for the behaviour outlined in the preceding paragraph. Now, in this chapter, we shall examine the methodological viewpoint of the historian of science Thomas S. Kuhn (as presented in Kuhn [1962]), which also offers an explanation of non-falsificationist behaviour. As noted in Chapter 1, while Kuhn's work actually preceded that of Lakatos, we have deliberately left the discussion of Kuhnian methodology to this point so as to provide an uninterrupted emphasis on the falsificationist and Lakatosian methodological viewpoints.

Occasional scientific revolutions rather than revolution in permanence

Before proceeding to examine Kuhn's methodology in detail, let us briefly note how the Kuhnian view of science differs from that of the falsificationist. As noted in Chapter 4, the falsificationist views science as progressing via the trial and error sequence involved in the continuous, repetitive process of proposing tentative theories and then rigorously testing these theories with the aim of eventually falsifying and replacing them by other tentative theories. In other words, the falsificationist views the scientific pattern as one of permanent revolution, with researchers continuously overthrowing and attempting to overthrow existing theories.

In contrast to this, Kuhn views the pattern of science as being composed of periods of non-revolutionary or *normal science*, occasionally interrupted by periods of revolutionary or *extraordinary science* leading to scientific revolutions and the establishment of new periods of normal science. Hence, during a period of Kuhnian normal science, researchers are viewed as contentedly accepting a set of basic theories (or a theoretical framework) rather than continuously attempting to overthrow or falsify these theories. It is only when a scientific revolution occurs that these theories are overthrown and replaced, and even here Kuhn argues that the overthrow of the old and the acceptance of the new set of theories cannot be adequately explained in falsificationist terms.

9.1 NORMAL SCIENCE: RESEARCH WORK WITHIN THE CONFINES OF A GENERALLY-ACCEPTED, DOMINANT PARADIGM

In a Kuhnian normal science period, research work is viewed as taking place within the context of a generally-accepted, dominant *paradigm*. While Kuhn's notion of paradigm is difficult to define precisely, a Kuhnian paradigm can be regarded as a conceptual framework which supplies researchers with (a) a perspective for viewing the world, (b) a common view of those features (such as logical consistency, predictive accuracy, broadness of scope, simplicity and fertility) that should characterize a good theory (even though Kuhn explicitly recognizes that individual researchers may apply different weights to these features in practice), (c) a theoretical framework for analysing problems, and (d) a set of techniques for empirically testing theoretical predictions.

The characteristic feature of Kuhnian normal science is that it portrays research work as being carried out by a scientific community that is in general agreement, not only with regard to the fundamental assumptions that underlie theoretical analysis, but also with regard to both the research problems that need to be solved and the theories and techniques that are to be utilized in attempts to solve these problems. This consensus within the scientific community means that fundamental assumptions are not questioned during a normal science period, but are only applied in the process of explanation and prediction. Consequently, the scientific community is free to concentrate its effort on the further articulation and application of the prevailing theoretical framework, rather than on producing fundamental novel changes in this framework.

Puzzle-solving rather than theory-testing

Kuhn recognizes that no paradigm ever completely resolves all its research problems, which means that a paradigm will always manifest an incomplete and imperfect match or fit between theory and observation. However, it is important to note that in Kuhnian normal science these anomalies, or discrepancies between theory and observation, are *not* treated as falsifying counterinstances to the prevailing paradigm. Rather, these anomalies are seen as challenging *puzzles* to be solved by further articulation of the existing theoretical framework.

During Kuhnian normal science the prevailing paradigm is implicitly accepted as a suitable basis for research work and, in addition, it is implicitly accepted that further ingenious articulation of the existing theoretical framework will be successful in eliminating any apparent anomaly. In other words, it is essentially this implicit acceptance of the paradigm which permits anomalies to be viewed as puzzles rather than as falsifying counterinstances. Consequently, while normal science will involve research work that is aimed at improving the theory/observation fit, and while this work will, in turn, involve empirical testing to check this improved fit, it must be noted that this testing is *not* viewed as an attempt to either confirm or falsify existing theories. Rather this testing is viewed as a way of checking whether or not a proposed puzzle solution is successful, *while still maintaining implicit trust in the prevailing paradigm.*

If a researcher attempts to solve some puzzle by a further articulation of existing theories, and if this conjectured puzzle solution fails when empirically tested, this failure is not taken as an indication of the inadequacy of the prevailing paradigm but rather as an indication of the researcher's inability to solve this puzzle. In other words, while empirical tests are carried out during normal science, these tests are not viewed as tests of current theories but rather as tests of the puzzle-solving ability of researchers. When an empirical test indicates that a proposed puzzle solution has failed it is the researcher who is discredited and not the current theoretical framework.

Efficiency of normal science

Since during a normal science period researchers implicitly accept the fundamental assumptions underlying the prevailing paradigm, this means that they can concentrate their research efforts on extending the existing theoretical framework rather than challenging or re-examining its basic assumptions. Hence, instead of engaging in the difficult and costly business of starting afresh, researchers are free to undertake more precise, esoteric work within the existing theoretical framework. According to Kuhn, this concentration of research effort will, in turn, result in both more efficient and more rapid progress in puzzle-solving.

Thus, during a normal science period, researchers are encouraged to do theoretical work which will not only improve the match between theory and observation, but will also increase the precision of existing applications of the current theoretical framework and lead to new applications. This theoretical development will, in turn, encourage the development of those mathematical techniques that are required for making new theoretical applications or refinements. In addition, researchers are encouraged to extend and improve the data collection and empirical work that goes alongside this theoretical development. This empirical development will, in turn, encourage the development of those statistical techniques that are required for improving the process of empirical testing.

Progress within a normal science period

By this stage of our discussion of Kuhnian normal science, it should be clear that normal science research activity is not directed towards the goal of producing major substantive novelties or fundamental changes in the basic assumptions underlying the prevailing paradigm's theoretical framework. Rather normal science research activity has as its aim the steady, cumulative extension of the precision and applicability of the existing theoretical framework. Consequently, in a Kuhnian normal science period, progress is defined in terms of puzzle-solving advances within the context of the prevailing paradigm. Moreover, in Kuhn's view, the suppression of fundamental novelties (resulting from the implicit acceptance of the basic assumptions underlying the existing paradigm) is an important aid in securing efficient, rapid progress in puzzle-solving.

The regulative influence of the paradigm

According to Kuhn, normal science research activity takes place against a background of implicit acceptance of the prevailing paradigm. Since this means that researchers implicitly accept the worldview embodied in the basic assumptions of the paradigm's theoretical framework, then the paradigm will exert a regulative influence on theoretical work in the sense that the paradigm will both suggest a certain range of theoretical possibilities and, by implication, rule out a range of other theoretical possibilities. Consequently, Kuhn views a paradigm as being able to guide research in the sense that the worldview and state of theoretical and empirical knowledge, constituting a paradigm, together define the puzzles to be solved and restrict the range of acceptable solutions to these puzzles. Moreover, as with the suppression of fundamental novelties, it is Kuhn's view that the restricted vision which results from the regulative influence of the prevailing paradigm enhances, rather than hinders, progress in puzzle-solving.

9.2 CRISIS, REVOLUTIONARY SCIENCE AND SCIENTIFIC REVOLUTION

In Kuhn's account, normal science or puzzle-solving is that activity in which most researchers spend most of their time. However, according to Kuhn, there may be times when researchers are faced with unexpected and persistent failures in puzzle-solving. In other words, whereas the scientific community expects certain anomalies to be eventually resolved by further development of the existing paradigm, these anomalies may remain despite repeated efforts to accommodate them within the prevailing paradigm.

Crisis

If these anomalies are such that they call into question the fundamental assumptions underlying the prevailing paradigm's theoretical framework, and if these anomalies continue to remain unresolved despite attempts by leading researchers to resolve them, then the scientific community will increasingly come to recognize that these anomalies represent a serious *crisis* for the prevailing paradigm. It is important to note, however, that the existence of persistent anomalies may not always induce a crisis. Essentially it is only when the anomalies threaten the paradigm's basic assumptions, and resist the attempts of eminent researchers to resolve them, that they gradually take on the character of crisis-provoking anomalies.

According to Kuhn, as the crisis deepens, researchers will begin to lose confidence in the prevailing paradigm. These doubts about the adequacy of the existing paradigm will, in turn, manifest themselves in debates over the appropriateness of the basic assumptions underlying the paradigm's theoretical framework. In addition, researchers will begin to consider alternatives to existing theories. In Kuhnian terminology, as the crisis deepens, normal science research activity begins to break down and to be replaced by revolutionary or *extraordinary science* research activity.

Extraordinary science

Before the crisis, researchers attempt to resolve anomalies by non-*ad hoc* modifications of the theoretical framework of the existing paradigm. However, as the crisis is recognized and becomes more acute, researchers begin to consider theoretical formulations which are completely unconstrained by the existing paradigm—the type of research activity which Kuhn terms *extraordinary science*. Hence, instead of normal science research activity within the confines of the existing paradigm, the crisis generates a period of extraordinary science research activity characterized by a proliferation of competing theories aimed at resolving the persistent anomalies.

The initial stages of the extraordinary science period will be characterized by conjectured solutions to the anomaly problem which only diverge from the existing paradigm in minor ways. However, as the anomalies persist, the conjectured solutions become more divergent. Consequently, during extraordinary science, while there is still a paradigm, Kuhn argues that the proliferation of competing, divergent articulations of this paradigm will lead to a blurring of both the paradigm and the rules of normal science puzzle-solving, in the sense that there will be less and less unanimity within the scientific community with regard to the legitimacy or otherwise of these articulations.

According to Kuhn, this period of extraordinary science will bring the crisis state to a close in one of three ways: (1) normal science will eventually succeed in resolving the crisis-provoking anomalies by further (non-divergent) articulation of the existing paradigm; (2) if the anomalies persist despite the proliferation of competing, divergent articulations of the existing paradigm, researchers set the problem aside for consideration by a future generation of researchers equipped with more advanced theoretical and empirical tools; (3) a new paradigm emerges in competition with the existing paradigm and is eventually accepted as a replacement for the existing paradigm—this transition from a crisis-ridden paradigm to a new paradigm constitutes what Kuhn calls a *scientific revolution*. In the next sub-section, we shall examine this third way of ending a crisis in more detail.

Scientific revolution

In the Kuhnian account, a new paradigm is viewed as emerging during the period of extraordinary science to compete with the existing paradigm. Rather than viewing the emergence of this new paradigm as a long, evolutionary process, Kuhn views the initial articulation of the new paradigm (or, at least, the initial ideas or hints which enable it to be articulated later) as emerging all at once in a flash of inspiration in the mind of a researcher.

Since the majority of the scientific community are already committed to the old paradigm (in the sense that they implicitly accept it as a suitable basis for research activity), despite the doubts raised by the crisis-provoking anomalies, the new paradigm will only be viewed as a serious candidate for replacing the old paradigm if it can make some claim to superiority. If the new paradigm can make such a claim, for example in terms of its ability to resolve the crisis-provoking anomalies and its promise of future success in problem-solving, then the scientific community will enter a period of debate over the relative superiority of the competing paradigms.

As this debate gets under way, a small minority of the scientific community will transfer allegiance to the new paradigm while the large majority will remain committed to the old paradigm (in the expectation that further articulation of this paradigm will eventually enable it to meet successfully the challenges of the new paradigm). Consequently, the scientific community will split into two groups containing the proponents of the respective, rival paradigms.

According to Kuhn, the ensuing debate over the relative problem-solving abilities of the competing paradigms will *not* be resolved by an appeal to the theoretical and empirical successes of each paradigm, but rather by persuasion and by increasing numbers of the scientific community being converted to allegiance to the new paradigm.

To explain why this is so, Kuhn argues that the competing paradigms are *incommensurable* which, in turn, inevitably means that the proponents of each paradigm will subscribe to very different basic assumptions and values and hence will always be arguing, to some extent, at cross-purposes with each other. Essentially Kuhn is claiming that the shift in meaning between the two paradigms is so extreme that the concepts contained in the theoretical framework of one paradigm cannot be expressed in terms of the other and therefore paradigms cannot be compared. Hence, Kuhn argues that since the proponents of each paradigm operate with a different set of basic assumptions (or worldview), and a different view not only of the significance of problems that ought to be resolved but also of the procedures and solutions that are appropriate or meaningful, then the superiority of one paradigm over the other cannot be *conclusively* resolved via logical argument. Consequently, in Kuhn's view, the debate over the superiority of the competing paradigms will ultimately be resolved via persuasion and conversion rather than by logical argument alone.

In the early stages of a scientific revolution, Kuhn envisages a few researchers deciding to embrace the new paradigm even though, at this point in time, it is neither fully articulated nor has it adequately demonstrated its problem-solving ability. Exactly why these researchers make this decision is hard to pin down, but their transfer of allegiance to the new paradigm amounts to a statement of faith in the new paradigm's promise of future success in problem-solving. As these supporters of the new paradigm begin to articulate it further, and explore its problem-solving ability, more researchers will be converted to allegiance to the new paradigm. With the continuation of this process, more and more researchers will transfer allegiance to the new paradigm until eventually the new paradigm replaces the old with practically all members of the scientific community now working within the framework of the new paradigm. At this stage, research work within the confines of the new paradigm becomes accepted as the new way of practising normal science and the scientific revolution is complete.

It is important to note, in the preceding paragraph, that Kuhn views the transfer of allegiance from the old paradigm to the new one, by individual researchers, as a conversion experience resembling a gestalt switch. In other words, since Kuhn argues that logical argument cannot *conclusively* demonstrate the superiority of one paradigm over another, he then further argues that psychological and sociological factors must be introduced in order to try to explain why members of the scientific community are persuaded to transfer allegiance from the old paradigm to the new one.

9.3 REVOLUTIONS AND SCIENTIFIC PROGRESS

Now that we have outlined Kuhn's account of a scientific revolution, we must ask the important question: does the transition to the new paradigm represent scientific progress in the sense that the new paradigm is a better approximation to the truth? Kuhn's answer is an unambiguous no. He argues that, since the new paradigm is incommensurable with the preceding old paradigm, there are no objective paradigm-independent standards that can be used to assess whether or not the new paradigm is a better approximation to the truth.

In Kuhn's account of paradigm change, the new paradigm replaces the old paradigm because this is what the scientific community chooses to do. But this community decision does not result from the application of objective appraisal criteria which enable the theories embedded in the rival paradigms to be objectively compared against each other and against empirical evidence. As pointed out in the previous sub-section, while the scientific community *does* consider the theoretical and empirical successes of competing paradigms, it is Kuhn's view that the logical argument resulting from such consideration is not sufficient to demonstrate the superiority of one paradigm over the other. Consequently, according to Kuhn, the explanation of paradigm choice, and hence of why the new paradigm has replaced the old paradigm, must ultimately be located in the psychological and sociological make-up of the scientific community. In other words, to understand paradigm change, Kuhn argues that we need to understand the nature of the scientific community in the sense of investigating its values and hence what it will and will not accept.

It is important to note that, despite the above discussion, Kuhn still claims that he is a convinced believer in scientific progress. Although Kuhn has argued that the application of objective appraisal criteria cannot conclusively establish that a paradigm is better than its predecessor, he nonetheless argues that the evolution of the scientific community's state of knowledge constitutes scientific progress. Consequently, Kuhn views more recently evolved paradigms as better than earlier paradigms for solving puzzles and for supporting the practice of normal science. Note, however, that Kuhn does not provide any objective criteria for assessing this claimed historical increase in puzzle-solving ability. In his account, the explanation of why the current, most-recently-evolved paradigm is regarded as possessing the highest puzzle-solving capacity must ultimately be found in the psychological and sociological make-up of the current scientific community.

The roles of normal and revolutionary science in scientific progress

Normal and revolutionary science play important roles in Kuhn's evolutionary account of scientific progress. During normal science the prevailing paradigm is implicitly accepted as an appropriate basis for research work and so researchers can concentrate their efforts on the further articulation of this paradigm, rather than challenging or re-examining its fundamental assumptions. As noted in Section 9.1, this essentially uncritical acceptance of the prevailing paradigm, during normal science, permits both more efficient and more rapid progress in puzzle-solving. However, not only does normal science encourage researchers to explore the potential of the existing paradigm fully, but normal science also tends to lead to a serious restriction of researchers' vision and thus to a considerable resistance by researchers to paradigm change. For Kuhn, this resistance to paradigm change represents an important aid to scientific progress rather than a serious hindrance.

Kuhn views the resistance to paradigm change as an important factor which prevents researchers from being too easily distracted and hence ensures that the existing paradigm will not be discarded before researchers have properly explored its potential. In addition, he argues that an anomaly can only be identified against the background provided by the existing paradigm. Hence, the more developed the existing paradigm, and the stronger the resistance to paradigm change, then the more precise will be the identification of both crisis-provoking anomalies and the need for paradigm change.

Once normal science has fulfilled its crucial role of isolating serious anomalies, and of highlighting the need for paradigm change, then normal science research activity begins to break down. The extraordinary or revolutionary science which replaces normal science then performs the important function of generating competing alternatives to existing theories, with a view to resolving the serious anomalies. As we have seen in Section 9.2, it is out of this process of competition that the new paradigm emerges and eventually the scientific revolution takes place. Consequently, in the Kuhnian account, both normal science and revolutionary science are essential to scientific revolutions and evolutionary scientific progress.

Before leaving this section, it is important to note that while Kuhn's account of scientific progress is essentially *descriptive* (in that it provides an historical description of scientific behaviour), it also has *prescriptive* implications. Thus, since Kuhn views normal science as highly beneficial (in the sense that it not only ensures substantial advances in puzzle-solving but also leads the way to scientific revolutions and hence to evolutionary scientific progress), then it follows that his methodological viewpoint has prescriptive implications for the way in which researchers should proceed in order to promote evolutionary scientific progress.

9.4 CRITICISMS OF KUHN

In this section we shall look briefly at some of the criticisms of

Kuhn's analysis and then, in the following section, we shall note some of the ways in which Lakatos's methodology has been influenced by Kuhn's work.

The vagueness of Kuhn's notion of a paradigm

As a starting point, recall that Kuhn's account tends to give the impression that the historical development of science consists of a sequence of discrete, clearly-defined paradigms. However, many writers have argued that Kuhn's notion of a paradigm is so vague and imprecise that it cannot usefully be applied in attempts to analyse and understand science. For example, one critic noted that Kuhn had actually used the term paradigm in twenty-one different senses.

However, while Kuhn's notion of a paradigm has been severely criticized, it has also been recognized that his characterization of paradigms has drawn attention to the need to analyse science in terms of theoretical frameworks rather than in terms of individual theories as in the inductivist, instrumentalist and falsificationist accounts.

The distinction between normal and revolutionary science

The Kuhnian account characterizes science as consisting of long periods of normal science research activity occasionally interrupted by periods of revolutionary science. Also, according to Kuhn, each normal science period is dominated by a single, ruling paradigm, so that competing paradigms only emerge during periods of revolutionary science. This characterization of science, with its stress on the crucial distinction between normal and revolutionary science, has however been criticized as descriptively inaccurate. Hence, some writers have argued that the history of science shows that competing paradigms are present all the time, and others have argued that science is characterized by continuous change rather than by occasional dramatic revolutions.

Kuhn also argued that normal science was beneficial in that it not only permitted substantial advances in puzzle-solving but also led the way to scientific revolutions. While critics have accepted that much research is characterized by an uncritical application of the theoretical framework of a dominant paradigm, they have argued that this normal science research activity does not enhance, but rather hinders, scientific progress. In particular, falsificationists have argued that a critical, undefensive approach, and hence a situation of permanent revolution, is much more beneficial to scientific progress.

The incommensurability of paradigms

In Sections 9.2 and 9.3, we noted how Kuhn views paradigms as incommensurable and how he concluded that the choice between competing paradigms must ultimately be explained in terms of the psychology and sociology of the scientific community, rather than in terms of the application of objective appraisal criteria. This incommensurability thesis, and the resorting to psychology and sociology to explain paradigm choice, has been heavily criticized. While critics do accept that there are difficulties in comparing paradigms, especially given that paradigm change usually involves both a loss as well as a gain in explanatory content, they argue that such comparison can still be made.

Moreover, they argue that such comparison can be made in terms of objective appraisal criteria rather than in terms of a subjective criterion such as Kuhn's 'consensus within the scientific community' with respect to a particular paradigm. Hence many critics argue that, despite content-comparison problems, there are adequate rational standards for assessing competing paradigms both against each other and against the empirical evidence, without having to resort to an investigation of the psychology and sociology of the relevant scientific community.

(Before proceeding, it should be noted that Kuhn not only has accepted many of the above criticisms but also has substantially changed his methodological position. However, in this chapter, we have only been concerned with elucidating the original Kuhnian position.)

9.5 KUHN'S INFLUENCE ON LAKATOS

A comparison of the methodologies of Kuhn and Lakatos would tend to support the view that Lakatos's work was influenced by that of Kuhn. Consequently, before leaving our discussion of Kuhn, we shall briefly list some of the instances of influence:

(1) Kuhn's work highlighted the need for a methodology that was able to counter the criticisms of falsificationism arising out of

historical studies of how scientists actually behave in practice. Lakatos's work, in common with that of Kuhn, attempts to meet these specific criticisms.

(2) Just as Kuhn's notion of a paradigm emphasizes the need to analyse science in terms of theoretical frameworks or structures (rather than in terms of individual theories as in inductivism, instrumentalism, or falsificationism), so also Lakatos's notion of a research programme places the emphasis on theoretical frameworks rather than on individual theories.

(3) During Kuhnian normal science, researchers are viewed as accepting the basic assumptions underlying the theoretical framework of the prevailing paradigm. It would appear that this aspect of Kuhnian analysis influenced Lakatos's notion of a hard core of hypotheses underlying a research programme, with these hard core hypotheses being deemed irrefutable by methodological decision. Moreover, in contrast to falsificationism, where metaphysics has only an external-influence role, both Kuhn and Lakatos give metaphysics a central, internal explanatory role in their methodological analyses.

(4) Just as Kuhn's analysis indicated how a paradigm will exert a regulative influence on theoretical work, so also Lakatos's analysis indicates how the hard core of a research programme has a regulatory influence on theory construction. Consequently, both Kuhn and Lakatos emphasize the change in worldview that results, respectively, from paradigm change and from research programme change.

(5) Kuhn's analysis of the efficiency of normal science provides a rationale for not changing the fundamental assumptions underlying the theoretical framework of a paradigm. Lakatos's analysis contains a similar rationale for not modifying the hard core of a research programme.

(6) Kuhn views his normal science research activity as basically similar to Lakatos's notion of research work in the protective belt of a research programme.

(7) Kuhn's account pointed out that a paradigm will not only guide research but will also give rise to simultaneous research discoveries. While Lakatos's account also contains these features, it is our view that Lakatos provides more insight into these features by introducing his important concept of the positive heuristic of a research programme.

(8) The development of theoretical work, and of mathematical and statistical techniques, during Kuhnian normal science would seem to have influenced Lakatos's discussion of theoretical autonomy. However, once more Lakatos's concept of the heuristic power of a research programme gives important additional insight into these features of scientific development.
(9) Kuhn referred to a paradigm's promise of success in a rather vague manner. While Lakatos's analysis also incorporates the notion of future promise, his concept of the positive heuristic is utilized to give a somewhat more definite picture of what is meant by the future promise of a research programme.
(10) Kuhn views his notion of a crisis, and the attendant *ad hoc* modifications of existing theories, as more or less equivalent to Lakatos's degenerating phase of a research programme.

Important differences between Kuhn and Lakatos

While the preceding sub-section lists important instances of Kuhn's influence on Lakatos, it is also important to note some of the major differences between the Kuhnian and Lakatosian approaches.

Perhaps the most immediate important difference between Kuhn and Lakatos relates to the question of objectivity. Thus, whereas Lakatos provides objective appraisal criteria for comparing rival research programmes at a given point in time, Kuhn not only does not attempt to provide such criteria but also argues that objective appraisal criteria could not provide a conclusive comparative evaluation of competing theoretical frameworks. Hence, while Lakatos's account relies only upon objective appraisal criteria, Kuhn explicitly introduces subjective factors by resorting to sociology and psychology in order to explain paradigm change.

Another important difference relates to the question of competing paradigms (or research programmes). Whereas in the Kuhnian account competing paradigms only appear during the period of revolutionary science (since, during normal science, the prevailing paradigm has a monopoly position), in Lakatos's account competing research programmes are viewed as both a necessary and ever-present feature of science.

Finally, it is important to note that Lakatos does not subscribe to Kuhn's incommensurability thesis. While Lakatos's work recognizes that there are difficulties in comparing research programmes, it is nonetheless accepted that objective comparison can be made at a given point in time. In addition, in contrast to Kuhn, Lakatos conjectured that the temporal sequence of progressive research programmes is likely to produce theories which are ever closer approximations to the truth.

9.6 KUHNIAN METHODOLOGY AND ECONOMICS

It is our opinion that MSRP is superior to Kuhnian methodology in providing important insights into the methodological problems associated with assessing the growth of economic knowledge.

Essentially we feel that MSRP has made an important contribution by incorporating, and improving upon, many of Kuhn's key insights without having to resort to non-objective explanatory factors. Also, as our discussion of the orthodox and Marxist economics research programmes in Chapter 8 has indicated, we view economics as being characterized by competing research programmes rather than by one paradigm. Consequently, given this view, we consider that it would be both inappropriate and descriptively inaccurate to apply Kuhn's methodology to economics.

(It is important to note that Kuhn envisaged the early stages of development of a science as being characterized by continual competition between rival worldviews and hence by continual competition between different ways of practising science. However, at this immature stage of development, the science does not possess a paradigm. In Kuhn's view, it is only when the science acquires a paradigm, and is therefore enabled to engage in the more esoteric type of research activity that he calls normal science, that the science can be regarded as mature. While Kuhn expressed no definite view as to whether the specific social science of economics should be classed as mature or immature, it is our view that economics can be classed as mature in the sense that paradigms, or research programmes, which permit the type of more esoteric research work that characterizes Kuhnian normal science, can indeed be identified. In holding this view, however, it should be obvious that we recognize that there is a very great difference between the maturity of, say, physics and the maturity of economics.)

In addition, while we accept that there have been important changes within both the orthodox and Marxist economics research programmes over time (and we also recognize that it is not uncommon for economists to call some of these changes 'revolutions'), we are not aware of any major changes in economics that could be accurately described as scientific revolutions in the Kuhnian sense. Finally, while we accept that there are difficulties in comparing the content of competing research programmes in economics, we do not subscribe to Kuhn's incommensurability thesis.

9.7 SUMMARY

Kuhn views the pattern of science as being composed of periods of non-revolutionary or normal science occasionally interrupted by periods of revolutionary or extraordinary science.

During Kuhnian normal science the prevailing paradigm is implicitly accepted as an adequate basis for research work. Hence, rather than questioning the basic assumptions underlying the prevailing paradigm's theoretical framework, researchers concentrate their efforts on solving the various research puzzles that arise when this framework is applied in order to produce explanations and predictions of the phenomena under consideration.

Occasionally researchers are faced with unexpected and persistent failures in puzzle-solving. If these failures to accommodate anomalies (via further articulation of the prevailing paradigm's theoretical framework) are such that they call into question the basic assumptions underlying the existing set of theories, then the scientific community will begin not only to doubt the adequacy of the existing paradigm but also to consider alternatives to existing theories. As this proliferation of alternative theories—or revolutionary research activity—continues, a new paradigm emerges and gradually wins the allegiance of more and more members of the scientific community. Eventually the new paradigm replaces the old and research work within the confines of the new paradigm becomes accepted as the new way of practising normal science. At this stage the scientific revolution is complete, with the explanation for the paradigm change being located in the sociological and psychological make-up of the scientific community.

In addition to arguing that the history of science is characterized by the above pattern of research activity, Kuhn also recommends that this pattern should be encouraged in order to promote scientific progress. Hence, he argues that normal science research activity should be encouraged not only so as to secure important advances in puzzle-solving but also to ensure that research activity leads to scientific revolutions and hence to scientific progress. Note, however, that for Kuhn scientific progress does not mean that a newly-accepted paradigm is a better approximation to the truth than its predecessor. Rather, given Kuhn's view of the incommensurability of paradigms, Kuhn only speaks of evolutionary scientific progress, with the most-recently-evolved paradigm being subjectively regarded by the scientific community as possessing the highest puzzle-solving capacity.

References for further reading

Kuhn's original position is presented in Kuhn [1962]. Modifications and development of Kuhn's position can be found in Kuhn [1970a], [1970b], [1970c], [1971], [1977a] and [1977b]. Musgrave [1971], and Toulmin [1972], pp. 98-117, provide discussions of changes in Kuhn's position.

Critical discussion of Kuhn, from a philosophy of science viewpoint, can be found in Blaug [1980a], pp. 29-33; Caldwell [1982], pp. 68-79; Chalmers [1982], Chapters 8 and 9; Feyerabend [1970]; Lakatos [1970], pp. 177-80; Laudan [1977], Chapters 3, 4 and 7; Masterman [1970]; Musgrave [1973]; Newton-Smith [1981], Chapter 5; Popper [1970]; Scheffler [1967]; Shapere [1964]; Suppe [1977], pp. 135-51, 636-49; Toulmin [1970]; Watkins [1970]; and Wisdom [1987a], Chapters 7 and 8.

For discussions of Kuhnian methodology and economics see Blaug [1973]; Bronfenbrenner [1971]; Coats [1969]; Dow [1985]; Goodwin [1973]; Hicks [1976]; Hutchison [1976], [1978] and [1981a]; Johnson [1971]; Katouzian [1980], pp. 91-106; Kunin and Weaver [1971]; Leijonhufvud [1976] and Routh [1987].

10 Feyerabend's Methodological Anarchism

In previous chapters we examined various methodological viewpoints such as inductivism, instrumentalism, falsificationism, MSRP and Kuhn's methodology. Now, as a stark contrast to these methodological viewpoints, we shall consider Paul Feyerabend's *methodological anarchism* as presented in Feyerabend [1975a].

10.1 ANYTHING GOES: THE ONLY METHODOLOGICAL PRINCIPLE THAT DOES NOT INHIBIT SCIENTIFIC PROGRESS

Feyerabend points out that a perusal of the history of science quickly reveals that the development of science is an exceedingly complex matter. Given this complex history of science, he then argues that it is most unrealistic to expect that simple methodological rules or principles (such as 'base explanations and predictions on highly confirmed theories', 'only be concerned with the predictive accuracy of theories', 'take falsification seriously', 'avoid *ad hoc* modifications of hypotheses', 'appraise research programmes in terms of both their theoretical and empirical progression and their heuristic power', 'encourage normal science research activity', and so on) will be successful in providing an explanation of scientific development. Consequently, after looking at case studies from the history of science, Feyerabend concludes that existing methodological principles provide an inadequate account of the past development of science.

According to Feyerabend, there are so many factors which influence scientific change that it is vain to try to rely on a few simple methodological rules in order to explain that change. Moreover, he argues that since research activity is much more 'sloppy' and 'irrational' than portrayed in methodological accounts, and since historical research conditions are continually changing, *no* system of methodological rules can be found which will provide an adequate account of the historical development of science.

In addition to arguing that existing methodological principles are inadequate to explain theory choice in the history of science, Feyerabend also claims that the adoption and application of such methodological principles or rules is liable to *hinder* scientific development in the future. To support this claim, Feyerabend argues that while many features of research activity inevitably appear as 'sloppiness' and 'chaos' when compared to precise methodological procedures, these very features have an important function in the development of science. Consequently, he maintains that the adoption of precise methodological procedures would actually have the effect of hindering scientific progress in the sense that these procedures would remove the apparent 'sloppiness' and 'chaos', and thus the crucial adaptability, which serve as important preconditions for scientific progress.

Further to support his claim that adherence to rigid, pre-specified methodological procedures would hinder scientific progress, Feyerabend asserts that the history of science not only provides evidence that every methodological rule has been violated at some point in the development of science, but also that important scientific advances only took place after methodological rules had been deliberately broken and set aside. Hence, according to Feyerabend, there have been numerous occasions in science when it has been essential to bend, ignore, or deliberately contradict highly-regarded methodological rules in order to secure significant scientific advances.

Given his argument that methodological rules hinder rather than help scientific progress, Feyerabend concludes that there is only *one* methodological principle or rule that will not inhibit progress in science and that is the principle of *methodological anarchism* or the principle of '*anything goes*'. Since, in his view, the history of science demonstrates that all methodologies have their limitations, and since he argues from this that no system of methodological rules can be found to guide theory choice or to enhance scientific progress, Feyerabend concludes that the only rule that can be defended under *all* conditions and at *every* point in the development of science is that of 'anything goes'.

The response to Feyerabend's critique of scientific method

Feyerabend has come under considerable criticism for presenting existing methodological procedures as systems of absolutely rigid, binding, exceptionless rules that govern scientific research activity. Critics have pointed out that not only has no one ever expected methodological rules to have no limitations but also it is quite common to regard methodological rules as evolving over time. To require methodological principles to be applicable to *all* circumstances, at *every* stage in the development of science, is deliberately to rule out useful, but obviously not exceptionless, methodological principles in favour of an empty and vague principle such as 'anything goes'. Clearly such a requirement would permit even reasonably successful methodological rules to be rejected immediately by an appeal to any curiosity in the history of science.

In addition, critics have pointed out that it is not sufficient to present a few historical examples of situations in which some methodological rules were either ignored or contradicted and then conclude from these examples that all methodological rules constitute a hindrance to scientific progress. Since Feyerabend has not provided a criterion that would enable an assessment of whether or not a particular methodological rule constitutes a hindrance to scientific progress, he has no adequate grounds for asserting that any particular rule has actually operated as a hindrance. Moreover, Feyerabend has been criticized for claiming that methodological rules hinder scientific progress without providing evidence that such rules have actually hindered more often than they have helped.

Critics of Feyerabend readily accept that scientific research activity is complex, that any methodology has its limitations and, therefore, that no special method can either guarantee success or make success probable. They also accept that many factors influence scientific change. However, while they agree with Feyerabend on these points, they do not accept his conclusion that the only adequate methodological principle that can be defended is 'anything goes'. Rather they argue that while methodologies do not provide binding, unchanging rules, they do provide useful, general guiding principles. In addition, given the very substantial achievements of the physical sciences, they argue that it is more reasonable to hypothesize that there is something special about scientific method than to assume that scientific advance is the product of an 'anything goes' methodology.

10.2 INCOMMENSURABILITY, THEORY PROLIFERATION AND SCIENTIFIC PROGRESS

Feyerabend holds the view that the meanings of theoretical and observational terms are entirely dependent on the theoretical context in which they occur. In other words, theoretical and observational terms obtain their specific meaning by being part of a specific theory (where Feyerabend's use of the word 'theory' refers to *both* comprehensive theoretical frameworks, or research programmes, and less comprehensive theories). Given this view, Feyerabend claims that the difference in meaning between rival theories is so extreme that the theoretical and observational terms associated with one theory cannot be expressed in terms of the other and therefore rival theories cannot be logically compared via the application of objective appraisal criteria. Hence Feyerabend maintains that rival theories are *incommensurable*.

Given his incommensurability thesis, Feyerabend then stresses the importance of *theory proliferation* for scientific progress. Rather than following the rule of generating theories which are required to both incorporate and be consistent with existing highly-confirmed theories (with this rule being regarded by Feyerabend as both unnecessarily restrictive and often ignored in practice), Feyerabend argues that researchers should be encouraged to increase the number of alternative, mutually inconsistent theories.

According to Feyerabend, this proliferation of theories is essential for ensuring an adequate assessment of existing theories. Hence, on the one hand, it is quite possible that one of these rival theories, despite its incompatibility with existing theories, may eventually be developed so as to become more acceptable than any theory which may emerge out of the development of existing theories. On the other hand, even if the existing theories continue to be highly confirmed and the rival theories are refuted by relevant empirical evidence, the proliferation of alternative, conflicting theories has still served the important function of expanding the stock of empirical knowledge and thereby providing a richer appreciation of why the existing theories are regarded as acceptable bases for scientific explanation and prediction.

Feyerabend also argues that the development of alternative, conflicting theories may also advance scientific knowledge in the sense that this proliferation enables researchers to view existing well-established results from the perspective of a completely different theory and this, in turn, may enable them to detect previously unrecognized, indefensible assumptions in the existing, currently-most-accepted theories. Lastly, in keeping with his 'anything goes' methodology which removes all methodological constraints from researchers, Feyerabend argues that the proliferation of theories should be encouraged so as to increase the freedom of individual researchers.

In addition to encouraging researchers to proliferate theories, Feyerabend also encourages researchers to hold on to these theories tenaciously so that science will fully benefit from the vigorous confrontation of tenaciously held rival theories. Consequently, even though a theory is theoretically contrary to much more highly confirmed theories, it should not be lightly given up. Moreover, according to Feyerabend, it is quite legitimate to retain a theory even in the face of falsifying counterinstances. In his view, it is quite reasonable to respond to apparent refutations by rejecting the theory or by rejecting the refuting observations or by resorting to *ad hoc* hypotheses (in order to protect a theory from premature rejection while giving it time to develop into a more adequate form). Given his 'anything goes' methodology, and his claim that such strategies have advanced science in the past, Feyerabend maintains that any of these responses is perfectly legitimate.

Subjective explanation of scientific change

Since Feyerabend's incommensurability thesis means that it is no longer possible to logically compare theories, then how does Feyerabend explain choice between incommensurable theories? In other words, once objective appraisal criteria have been rejected, how are comparisons of theories to be made? Feyerabend's answer is that comparisons of theories and theory choice are essentially a matter of subjective preferences. Hence, for Feyerabend, scientific change is to be ultimately explained in *subjective* terms. (Note that Feyerabend's position is not exactly the same as Kuhn's position.

Kuhn does not reject objective appraisal criteria, rather he argues that the application of objective appraisal criteria cannot provide conclusive answers and thus the explanation for scientific change must be located in psychological and sociological factors.)

Feyerabend's methodological viewpoint does, however, permit objective appraisal within the confines of a *particular* theory. This means that a particular theory can be appraised not only in terms of its internal logical consistency but also in terms of the observational data associated with this theory. Consequently, within this context, Feyerabend allows for the possibility of a particular theory being either confirmed or refuted by empirical evidence. This, in turn, enables Feyerabend to talk of a particular theory improving its approximation to the truth. Note, however, that although his analysis permits such appraisal, Feyerabend is quick to point out that his incommensurability thesis has the effect of greatly reducing the usefulness of such appraisal.

While Feyerabend permits the above objective appraisal of particular theories, he is adamant that objective comparative appraisals of rival theories cannot be made due to the incommensurability of theories. Hence, according to Feyerabend, one cannot objectively compare the explanatory content and empirical success of rival theories or objectively appraise one theory as a better approximation to the truth than another. As noted above, comparisons of theories, theory choice and the assessment of scientific progress become a matter of subjective, individual judgement. In other words, in Feyerabend's account, the individual researcher has the freedom to choose and appraise theories, and thus assess the growth of scientific knowledge, according to his or her own subjective preferences (and Feyerabend's personal judgement is that science has greatly increased our understanding of the world and that this understanding has led to even greater practical achievements).

10.3 CRITICISMS OF FEYERABEND

Feyerabend's incommensurability thesis has given rise to considerable criticism. While philosophers of science accept that there are difficulties in comparing the content and performance of theories, they do not accept Feyerabend's extreme view that theories are incommensurable and therefore cannot be compared by the application of objective appraisal criteria. In particular, they do not accept Feyerabend's analysis of meaning which, as we saw above, implies that (except in trivial cases) the meaning of all theoretical and observational terms change as we move from one theory to another. Not only have critics put forward alternative analyses of meaning which do not imply incommensurability, but they have also shown that the history of science contains many counter-examples to Feyerabend's historical illustrations of incommensurability. Feyerabend has also been criticized for generalizing from a few historical examples to all cases. In addition, Feyerabend has also been criticized for not providing a specific analysis either of how a theory change actually leads to a change in the meaning of all terms or of how the influence of theory change on the meaning of terms is to be recognized.

The above criticisms of Feyerabend's incommensurability thesis indicate that Feyerabend has by no means established that research activity cannot be assessed and guided by objective appraisal criteria, but only by the subjective preferences of researchers. Also, while Feyerabend has claimed (and his critics agree) that many factors influence scientific change, this multiplicity of factors does not necessarily mean that an objective explanation of scientific change cannot be given.

Critics of Feyerabend have also pointed out that his incommensurability thesis is inconsistent with his views on theory proliferation. If theories are incommensurable as Feyerabend claims, then theory proliferation cannot aid the assessment of existing theories in the ways Feyerabend has suggested. Knowledge gained from an understanding of a rival theory clearly cannot tell us anything about an existing theory if these theories are incommensurable. It is one thing for Feyerabend to claim that theory proliferation and an 'anything goes' methodology aids scientific progress, but very much another thing to secure this progress if theories are incommensurable. In addition, Feyerabend's critics have also indicated that theory proliferation is not the only way to detect unrecognized implicit assumptions in existing theories. Such implicit assumptions could also be uncovered by a rigorous examination of existing theories.

While philosophers of science accept that theory proliferation and competition between tenaciously held theories can play an important role in scientific advance, they are unwilling to accept

Feyerabend's views on theory proliferation and tenacity. As noted in Section 10.2, Feyerabend's views encourage the proliferation of tenaciously held theories which need to be neither well-confirmed empirically nor theoretically consistent with well-established existing theories. In contrast to this 'anything goes' proliferation of theories, most philosophers of science only regard theory proliferation as useful if the theories are well supported both theoretically and empirically (which, for example, would be the case if these theories were theoretically and empirically progressive in the Lakatosian sense).

Moreover, while Feyerabend claims that the contradictions, inherent in proliferating theories that are both theoretically and empirically inconsistent with well-established theories, will operate in a dialectical fashion to produce advances in scientific knowledge, critics have pointed out that Feyerabend has not specified how these contradictions will be resolved. Consequently, it is far from obvious that his dialectical process will produce scientific advance.

Feyerabend's views on theory proliferation have also been criticized on the grounds that they give inadequate attention to the financial and institutional constraints on research activity. Thus, while Feyerabend has encouraged theory proliferation as a way of increasing the freedom of individuals, it clearly would be most inefficient for each individual researcher to be always trying to develop his or her own completely unique theory (or theoretical framework). Unlike Lakatos, Feyerabend has given little attention to the programmatic nature of research activity and thus to the costs involved in constantly changing the hard core and positive heuristic of a theoretical framework or research programme. Similarly, unlike Kuhn, Feyerabend has largely ignored the institutional research situation which makes Kuhnian normal science research activity possible. Moreover, within the institutional research situation, researchers are often operating as members of research teams rather than as autonomous individuals with the freedom to develop whatever theory they please.

Methodological anarchism and economics

Given that we agree with the foregoing criticisms of Feyerabend's methodological anarchism (and with the criticisms of both his incommensurability thesis and his views on theory proliferation), we feel that Feyerabend's 'anything goes' methodology would be inappropriate for economics. While we are aware that any of the methodologies discussed in earlier chapters of this book would have its limitations if applied to economics, we nonetheless contend that methodological principles can provide important insights into the complex problems of theory appraisal and theory choice in economics.

In addition, given that we have specifically argued that the adoption of MSRP in economics would give important insights into the complex research situation of economics, we also want to point out that we do not accept Feyerabend's view that Lakatos's MSRP is merely methodological anarchism in disguise. Essentially we feel that Feyerabend's criticism of MSRP errs in the sense that it follows the standard Feyerabend strategy of zoning in on one particular limitation of a methodology and then concluding from this that all methodological principles should be abandoned in favour of his 'anything goes' methodology. In other words, Feyerabend leaps from the fact that since MSRP not only recognizes that a degenerating research programme may stage a comeback, but also it provides no time limit for regarding such a research programme as being beyond reasonable hope of staging a comeback, then one must conclude that Lakatos's methodological viewpoint permits methodological anarchism. We do not accept that this conclusion is warranted.

As noted in Chapter 6, MSRP *does* provide objective appraisal criteria for evaluating one research programme as superior to another *at a given point in time*. Admittedly, MSRP also recognizes that this evaluation may be reversed in the future. However, while this is so, it is rather unrealistic to expect MSRP (or any other method of appraisal) to be able to provide a means whereby we could appraise the *future* performance of a research programme (though in Section 6.5 we noted how MSRP does enable one to make some, albeit limited, prediction of the potential for future development of a research programme). Consequently, if researchers wish to avail themselves of it, MSRP does provide useful objective criteria for appraising research activity at a specific point in time, and hence there is no need to accept Feyerabend's conclusion that researchers can only resort to subjective appraisals that are based on the subjective preferences and wishes of researchers. (For the view that economists have not only followed an 'anything goes' methodology in practice, but also that this is a good thing, see McCloskey [1983] and [1986].)

10.4 SUMMARY

Feyerabend argues that the development of science is so complex that no system of methodological rules can be found which would provide an adequate explanation of scientific change. According to Feyerabend, not only have all methodological rules been broken in the development of science but indeed this violation of methodological principles was and is necessary in order to secure scientific progress. Consequently, to avoid inhibiting scientific progress and to increase the freedom of individuals, Feyerabend proposes methodological anarchism or an 'anything goes' methodology.

Feyerabend also argues that theories are incommensurable and hence researchers should be encouraged to proliferate theories so that scientific advance can be enhanced via the interplay of tenaciously held rival theories. While Feyerabend holds that scientific advance has taken place, his incommensurability thesis means that objective comparative appraisals of rival theories cannot be made and hence, in his view, comparison of theories, theory choice and the assessment of scientific progress become a matter of subjective individual judgement, with this judgement being based, in turn, on the subjective preferences and wishes of individual researchers.

References for further reading

Feyerabend's methodological anarchism is presented in Feyerabend [1975a] and developed further in Feyerabend [1978]. Earlier presentations of Feyerabend's methodological viewpoint can be found in Feyerabend [1962], [1963], [1965] and [1970]. For a useful brief outline of Feyerabend's position, see Feyerabend [1975b].

Critical discussion of Feyerabend can be found in Achinstein [1964], [1968], Chapter 6; Ackermann [1976], Chapter 3; Blaug [1980a], pp. 40-4; Caldwell [1982], pp. 79-85; Chalmers [1982], Chapter 12; Giedymin [1971]; Hesse [1963]; Newton-Smith [1981], Chapter 6; Putman [1965]; Scheffler [1967], pp. 50-2; Shapere [1966]; and Suppe [1977], pp. 170-80, 636-49.

11 Concluding Comments

At this stage, it would be very pleasing if we were able to conclude, from the discussion in Chapters 2-10, that we have identified a methodology which provides us with objective appraisal criteria which, in turn, enable us to obtain *precise* answers to the important questions of how to appraise economic theories, compare economic theories and assess the growth of economic knowledge towards the goal of increasing verisimilitude. Unfortunately, we cannot easily reach such a conclusion. Rather, on the basis of the discussion in Chapters 2-10, we must conclude not only that we have not succeeded in identifying such a methodology, but also that it is an exceedingly difficult task to construct a methodology that is capable of providing such precise answers.

However, while this is so, it is our opinion that the difficulty in constructing such a methodology, and hence in obtaining such precise answers, constitutes in itself an important reason for introducing economics students to the methodological issues involved in assessing the growth of economic knowledge. We feel that an awareness of these methodological issues should be an essential part of the education of economics students, in order to protect them from the danger of excessive expectations, or excessive disillusionment, with respect to the claims of economic theories and the economic policy recommendations based on these theories.

In particular, it is our contention that an understanding of MSRP, and of the implications of adopting MSRP in economics, gives students considerable insight into the complexities of the research situation in economics. Not only are they made aware that certain periods of theoretical autonomy in economics are inevitable, but also they are made aware of just how difficult it is to assess the costs and benefits of such theoretical autonomy. This awareness, plus an awareness of the complex subject matter of economics and of the difficulties facing empirical work in economics, helps students to realize that it is much easier to voice the oft-repeated criticism that current economics is excessively theoretical, and call for greater emphasis on empirical analysis, than it is to remedy the situation. In other words, students are helped to realize that it is one thing to demand that economic explanations and policy recommendations should only be based on theories which have been highly confirmed by numerous, rigorous empirical tests, but very much another thing to achieve this in practice.

Moreover, we feel that an understanding of MSRP, and of the implications of adopting MSRP in economics, is essential in introducing students not only to the concept of research programmes (and subprogrammes) but also to the problems involved in comparing rival research programmes. As Chapter 8 has indicated, the adoption of MSRP can provide valuable insight into the many complexities that are involved in making a comparison of rival research programmes such as the orthodox and Marxist research programmes. In particular, it provides a most valuable insight by stressing that the theories, and hence the theoretical predictions and policy recommendations, produced by a given research programme are not only built around but also imply the specific metaphysics (or world picture) contained in that research programme's hard core. Consequently, as students are helped, via this MSRP insight, to see the explicit link between policy recommendations and a specific metaphysics (or world picture), it is much easier for them to see exactly why there may be considerable disagreement over policy matters.

In addition, when the comparison of rival research programmes is accompanied by an explanation of the differences between positive and normative analysis, as we have done in Chapter 8, students are made to realize that while the comparison of rival research programmes and rival policy recommendations is exceedingly complex there is still considerable scope for positive analysis in economics.

Finally, while we personally favour the adoption of a 'falsification-augmented MSRP' in economics (see Section 7.6), we are well aware that such a methodology also faces difficulties in providing precise answers to the important questions of theory appraisal, theory comparison, and assessment of the growth of economic knowledge. Also, as the discussion of Chapter 8 has indicated, we are well aware that MSRP (falsification-augmented or otherwise) faces difficulties when it comes to comparing rival research programmes and rival policy recommendations. Nonetheless, it is our contention that MSRP has important pedagogic value in the sense that it provides a useful framework for identifying where many of the complications involved in such comparisons are located. In other words, while we recognize that the adoption of MSRP will not solve all the exceedingly complex problems involved in comparing rival research programmes, we do feel that its adoption would help to clarify the often-muddled discussion which at present accompanies such comparisons.

References for further reading

For Lakatos's suggestion that an 'historical' method can be used to compare or evaluate rival methodologies see Lakatos [1971a]. Criticism of Lakatos's general method for appraising methodologies can be found in Hands [1985b] and in Newton-Smith [1981], pp. 92-7.

Bibliography

Aaronovitch, S. and Smith, R. (1981) *The Political Economy of British Capitalism : A Marxist Analysis*, London: McGraw-Hill.

Achinstein, P. (1964) 'On the Meaning of Scientific Terms', *Journal of Philosophy*, 61, pp. 475-510.

——— (1968) *Concepts of Science*, Baltimore: Johns Hopkins Press.

Ackermann, R.J. (1976) *The Philosophy of Karl Popper*, Amherst: University of Massachusetts Press.

Agassi, J. (1964) 'The Nature of Scientific Problems and their Roots in Metaphysics', pp. 189-211 in Bunge [1964].

——— (1975) *Science in Flux*, Dordrecht-Holland: Reidel.

Archibald, G.C. (1979) 'Method and Appraisal in Economics', *Philosophy of the Social Sciences*, 9, pp. 304-315.

Asquith, P.D. and Giere, R. (eds) (1980) *PSA 1980*, East Lansing, Mich.: Philosophy of Science Association.

——— and Kyburg, H.E. (eds) (1979) *Current Research in Philosophy of Science*, Philosophy of Science Association, Michigan.

Avineri, S. (1968) *The Social and Political Thought of Karl Marx*, Cambridge: Cambridge University Press.

Baumrin, B. (ed.) (1963) *Philosophy of Science. The Delaware Seminar*, Vol. II. New York: Interscience.

Begg, D.K.H. (1982) *The Rational Expectations Revolution in Macroeconomics*, Oxford : Philip Allan.

Berkson, W. (1976) 'Lakatos One and Lakatos Two: An Appreciation', pp. 39-54 in Cohen, Feyerabend, and Wartofsky [1976].

Black, R.D.C., Coats, A.W. and Goodwin, C.D.W. (eds) (1973) *The Marginal Revolution in Economics*, Durham: N.C.

Blaug, M. (1973) 'Was There a Marginal Revolution?', pp. 3-14 in Black, Coats, and Goodwin [1973].

——— (1976) 'Kuhn versus Lakatos, or paradigms versus research

programmes in the history of economics', pp. 149-80 in Latsis [1976].
——— (1980a) *The Methodology of Economics: Or How Economists Explain*, Cambridge: Cambridge University Press.
——— (1980b) *A Methodological Appraisal of Marxian Economics*, Amsterdam: North-Holland.
——— (1985) 'Comment on D. Wade Hands, "Karl Popper and Economic Methodology: A New Look"', *Economics and Philosophy*, 1, pp. 286-8.
Boland, L.A. (1979) 'A Critique of Friedman's Critics', *Journal of Economic Literature*, 17(2), pp. 503-22.
——— (1982) *The Foundations of Economic Method*, London: Allen and Unwin.
Bottomore, T. (ed.) (1983) *A Dictionary of Marxist Thought*, Oxford: Basil Blackwell.
Bronfenbrenner, M. (1971) 'The "Structure of Revolutions" in Economic Thought', *History of Political Economy*, 3, pp. 136-51.
Buck, R.C. and Cohen, R.S. (eds) (1971) *PSA 1970: In Memory of Rudolf Carnap, Boston Studies in the Philosophy of Science*, Vol. VIII. Dordrecht, Holland: Reidel.
Bunge, M. (1964) *The Critical Approach to Science and Philosophy*, New York: Free Press.

Caldwell, B.J. (1982) *Beyond Positivism: Economic Methodology in the Twentieth Century*, London: Allen and Unwin.
Chalmers, A.F. (1982) *What is This Thing Called Science?*, 2nd edn., Milton Keynes: Open University Press.
Coats, A.W. (1969) 'Is there a Structure of Scientific Revolutions in Economics?', *Kyklos*, 22, pp. 289-96.
Coddington, A. (1972) 'Positive Economics', *Canadian Journal of Economics*, 5, pp. 1-15.
——— (1975) 'The Rationale of General Equilibrium Theory', *Economic Inquiry*, 13, pp. 539-58.
Cohen, G.A. (1978) *Karl Marx's Theory of History: A Defence*, Oxford: Clarendon.
Cohen, R.S. and Wartofsky, M.W. (eds) (1965) *Boston Studies in the Philosophy of Science*, Vol. II. New York: Humanities Press.
——— Feyerabend, P.K. and Wartofsky, M.W. (eds) (1976) *Essays in Memory of Imre Lakatos. Boston Studies in the Philosophy of Science*, Vol. XXXIX. Dordrecht, Holland: Reidel.
Colodny, R. (ed.) (1966) *Mind and Cosmos : Explorations in the Philosophy of Science*, Pittsburgh: University of Pittsburgh Press.
Cross, R. (1982a) 'The Duhem-Quine Thesis, Lakatos and the Appraisal of Theories in Macroeconomics', *Economic Journal*, 92, pp. 320-40.

——— (1982b) *Economic Theory and Policy in the U.K.: An Outline and Assessment of the Controversies*, Oxford: Martin Robertson.

De Marchi, N. (1976) 'Anomaly and the development of economics: the case of the Leontief paradox', pp. 109-27 in Latsis [1976].
Dow, S.C. (1985) *Macroeconomic Thought: A Methodological Approach*, Oxford : Basil Blackwell.

Feigl, H. and Maxwell, G. (eds) (1962) *Minnesota Studies in the Philosophy of Science*, Vol. III. Minneapolis: University of 2Minnesota Press.
Feyerabend, P.K. (1962) 'Explanation, Reduction, and Empiricism', pp. 28-97 in Feigl and Maxwell [1962].
——— (1963) 'How to Be a Good Empiricist—A Plea for Tolerance in Matters Epistemological', pp. 3-20 in Baumrin [1963].
——— (1965) 'On the Meaning of Scientific Terms', *Journal of Philosophy*, 62, pp. 266-74.
——— (1970) 'Consolations for the Specialist', pp. 197-230 in Lakatos and Musgrave [1970].
——— (1975a) *Against Method: Outline of an Anarchistic Theory of Knowledge*, London: New Left Books.
——— (1975b) 'How to Defend Society Against Science', *Radical Philosophy*, 11, pp. 3-8.
——— (1978) *Science in a Free Society*, London: New Left Books.
Fine, B. (1980) *Economic Theory and Ideology*, London: Edward Arnold.
——— (1982) *Theories of the Capitalist Economy*, London: Edward Arnold.
——— (1984) *Marx's Capital*, 2nd edn., London: Macmillan.
——— and Harris, L. (1979) *Rereading Capital*, London: Macmillan.
Fisher, R.M. (1986) *The Logic of Economic Discovery: Neoclassical Economics and the Marginal Revolution*, Brighton: Wheatsheaf Books.
Friedman, M. (1953) 'The Methodology of Positive Economics', pp. 3-43 in Friedman [1953a].
——— (1953a) *Essays in Positive Economics*, Chicago: University of Chicago Press.

Giedymin, J. (1971) 'Consolations for the Irrationalist?', *British Journal for the Philosophy of Science*, 22, pp. 28-48.
——— (1976) 'Instrumentalism and Its Critiqu: A Reappraisal', pp. 179-207 in Cohen, Feyerabend, and Wartofsky [1976].
Gilbert, C.L. (1986) 'The Development of British Econometrics 1945-85', Applied Economics Discussion Paper 8, Institute of Economics

and Statistics, Oxford.
Glass, J.C. and Johnson, W. (1988) 'Metaphysics, MSRP and Economics', *British Journal for the Philosophy of Science* 39 (3), pp. 313-30.
Goodwin, C.D.W. (1973) 'Marginalism Moves to the New World', pp. 285-304 in Black, Coats, and Goodwin [1973].

Hahn, F. and Hollis, M (eds) (1979) *Philosophy and Economic Theory*, Oxford: Oxford University Press.
Hands, D.W. (1979) 'The Methodology of Economic Research Programmes', *Philosophy of the Social Sciences*, 9, pp. 293-303.
——— (1984) 'Blaug's Economic Methodology', *Philosophy of the Social Sciences*, 14, pp. 115-25.
——— (1985a) 'Karl Popper and Economic Methodology', *Economics and Philosophy*, 1, pp. 83-99.
——— (1985b) 'Second Thoughts on Lakatos', *History of Political Economy*, 17:1, pp. 1-16.
Harding, S.G. (ed.) (1976) *Can Theories be Refuted*? Dordrecht, Holland: Reidel.
Hausman, D.M. (1980) 'How to do Philosophy of Economics', pp. 353-62 in Asquith and Giere [1980].
——— (1981) 'Are General Equilibrium Theories Explanatory?', pp. 17-32 in Pitt [1981].
Hesse, M. (1963) 'A New Look at Scientific Explanation', *Review of Metaphysics*, 17, pp. 98-108.
Hicks, J.R. (1976)' "Revolutions" in Economics', pp. 207-18 in Latsis [1976].
Howard, M.C. and King, J.E. (1985) *The Political Economy of Marx*, 2nd edn., London: Longman.
Hunt, E.K. (1979) *History of Economic Thought: A Critical Perspective*, Belmont, California: Wadsworth.
Hutchison, T.W. (1964) *'Positive' Economics and Policy Objectives*, London: Allen and Unwin.
——— (1976) 'On the History and Philosophy of Science and Economics', pp. 181-205 in Latsis [1976].
——— (1978) *On Revolutions and Progress in Economic Knowledge*, Cambridge : Cambridge University Press.
——— (1981a) *The Politics and Philosophy of Economics*, Oxford : Basil Blackwell.
———(1981b) 'On the Aims and Methods of Economic Theorizing', pp. 266-307 in Hutchison [1981a].

Johnson, H.G. (1971) 'The Keynesian revolution and the monetarist

counter-revolution', *American Economic Review*, 61, pp. 1-14.
Junankar, P.N. (1982) *Marx's Economics*, Oxford: Philip Allan.

Katouzian, H. (1980) *Ideology and Method in Economics*, London: Macmillan.

Kirzner, I.M. (ed.) (1982) *Method, Process, and Austrian Economics: Essays in Honor of Ludwig von Mises*, Mass.: Lexington.
Klappholz, K. (1964) 'Value Judgements and Economics', *British Journal for the Philosophy of Science*, 15, pp. 97-114.
Koertge, N. (1971) 'Inter-Theoretic Criticism and the Growth of Science', pp. 160-73 in Buck and Cohen [1971].
——— (1975) 'Popper's Metaphysical Research Program for the Human Sciences', *Inquiry*, 19, pp. 437-62.
——— (1978) 'Towards a New Theory of Scientific Inquiry', pp. 253-78 in Radnitzky and Andersson [1978].
——— (1979a) 'Does Social Science Really Need Metaphysics?' English translation (kindly provided by N. Koertge) of 'Braucht die Sozialwissenschaft wirklich Metaphysick' in *Theorie und Erfahrung*, Albert, H. and Stapf, K.H. (eds), (1979), Stuttgart: Klett-Cotta, pp. 55-81.
——— (1979b) 'The Problem of Appraising Scientific Theories', pp. 228-51 in Asquith and Kyburg [1979].
——— (1981) 'Ideology, Science and a Free Society', English translation (kindly provided by N. Koertge) of 'Ideologie, Wissenschaft und eine freie Gesellschaft', *Versuchungen Aufsatze zur Philosophie Paul Feyerabends, 2. Band*, Duerr, H.P. (ed.), (1981), Frankfurt: Suhrkamp Verlag, pp. 95-115.
Kuhn, T.S. (1962) *The Structure of Scientific Revolutions*, Chicago: University of Chicago Press.
——— (1970a) 'Logic of Discovery or Psychology of Research', pp. 1-23 in Lakatos and Musgrave [1970].
——— (1970b) 'Reflections on My Critics', pp. 231-78 in Lakatos and Musgrave [1970].
——— (1970c) *The Structure of Scientific Revolutions*, 2nd edn., enlarged, Chicago: University of Chicago Press.
——— (1971) 'Notes on Lakatos', pp. 137-46 in Buck and Cohen [1971].
——— (1977a) 'Second Thoughts on Paradigms', pp. 459-82 in Suppe [1977].
——— (1977b) *The Essential Tension*, Chicago: University of Chicago Press.
Kunin, L. and Weaver, F.S. (1971) 'On the Structure of Scientific Revolutions in Economics', *History of Political Economy*, 3, pp. 391-7.

Lakatos, I. (ed.) (1968a) *The Problem of Inductive Logic*', Amsterdam: North Holland.

——— (1968b) 'Changes in the Problem of Inductive Logic', pp. 315-417 in Lakatos [1968a].

(1970) 'Falsification and the Methodology of Scientific Research Programmes', pp. 91-196 in Lakatos and Musgrave [1970].

——— (1971a) 'History of Science and its Rational Reconstructions', pp. 91-136 in Buck and Cohen [1971].

——— (1971b) 'Replies to Critics', pp. 174-82 in Buck and Cohen [1971].

——— (1978) *Philosophical Papers*, 2 volumes, Worrall, J. and Currie, G. (eds), Cambridge: Cambridge University Press.

——— (1978a) 'Science and Pseudoscience', pp. 1-7 in Worrall and Currie [1978].

———and Musgrave, A. (eds) (1970) *Criticism and the Growth of Knowledge*, Cambridge: Cambridge University Press.

Latsis, S.J. (1976) *Method and Appraisal in Economics*, Cambridge: Cambridge University Press.

———(1976a) 'A research programme in economics', pp. 1-41 in Latsis [1976].

Laudan, L. (1977) *Progress and its Problems*, London: Routledge & Kegan Paul.

Lawson, T. (1985) 'Uncertainty and Economic Analysis', *Economic Journal*, 95, pp. 909-27.

Leijonhufvud, A. (1976) 'Schools, "Revolutions" and Research Programmes in Economic Theory', pp. 65-108 in Latsis [1976].

Leontief, W. (1971) 'Theoretical Assumptions and Nonobserved Facts', *American Economic Review*, 61, pp. 1-7.

——— (1982) 'Academic Economics', letter in *Science*, 217, pp. 104-7.

Levine, A. and Wright, E.O. (1980) 'Rationality and Class Struggle', *New Left Review*, 123, pp. 47-68.

Loasby, B.J. (1984) 'On Scientific Method', *Journal of Post Keynesian Economics*, Vol. VI, 3, pp. 394-410.

Losee, J. (1980) *A Historical Introduction to the Philosophy of Science*, 2nd edn., Oxford: Oxford University Press.

Marx, K. (1970) *Capital*, 3 vols., Moscow: Foreign Languages Publishing House (vol. I, 1970; vol. II, 1967; vol III, 1971).

——— (1973) *Grundrisse*, Harmondsworth: Penguin.

Masterman, M. (1970) 'The Nature of a Paradigm', pp. 59-89 in Lakatos and Musgrave [1970].

McCloskey, D.N. (1983) 'The Rhetoric of Economics', *Journal of*

Economic Literature, Vol. XXI, pp. 481-517.
——— (1986) *The Rhetoric of Economics*, Brighton: Wheatsheaf Books.
McLellan, D. (1973) *Karl Marx : His Life and Thoughts*, London: Macmillan.
McMullin, E. (1978) 'Philosophy of Science and its Rational Reconstructions', pp. 221-52 in Radnitzky and Andersson [1978].
——— (1979) 'The Ambiguity of "Historicism"', pp. 55-83 in Asquith and Kyburg [1979].
Miller, M.H. (1971) 'Estimates of the static balance of payments and welfare costs of United Kingdom entry into the Common Market', *National Institute Economic Review*, 57, pp. 69-83.
——— and Spencer, J.E. (1977) 'The static economic effects of the UK joining the EEC: a general equilibrium approach', *Review of Economic Studies*, 44, pp. 71-93.
Musgrave, A. (1971) 'Kuhn's Second Thoughts', *British Journal or the Philosophy of Science*, 22, pp. 207-45.
——— (1973) 'Falsification and its Critics', pp. 393-406 in Suppes *et al.* [1973].
——— (1976) 'Method or Madness?', pp. 457-91 in Cohen, Feyerabend and Wartofsky [1976].
——— (1978) 'Evidential Support, Falsification, Heuristics, and Anarchism', pp. 181-201 in Radnitzky and Andersson [1978].

Newton-Smith, W.H. (1981) *The Rationality of Science*, London: Routledge & Kegan Paul.
Ng, Yew-Kwang (1972) 'Value judgements and economists' role in policy recommendation', *Economic Journal*, 82, pp. 1014-18.
——— (1983) *Welfare Economics*, revised ed., London: Macmillan.

O'Brien, D.P. (1975) 'Whither Economics?', *Economics*, 11, 2, pp. 75-98.
——— (1983) 'Research Programmes in Competitive Structure', *Journal of Economic Studies*, 10, 4, pp. 29-51.
O'Hear, A. (1980) *Karl Popper*, London: Routledge & Kegan Paul.

Pitt, J.C. (ed.) (1981) *Philosophy in Economics*, Dordrecht : Reidel.
Popper, K.R. (1959) *The Logic of Scientific Discovery*, London: Hutchinson.
——— (1970) 'Normal Science and its Dangers', pp. 51-8 in Lakatos and Musgrave [1970].
——— (1972a) *Objective Knowledge*, London: Oxford University Press.
——— (1972b) 'Conjectural Knowledge: My Solution of the Problem of Induction', pp. 1-31 in Popper [1972a].

——— (1972c) 'The Bucket and the Searchlight: Two Theories of Knowledge', pp. 341-61 in Popper [1972a].

——— (1972d) *Conjectures and Refutations: The Growth of Scientific Knowledge*, 4th edn., London: Routledge & Kegan Paul.

Putnam, H. (1965) 'How not to talk about Meaning', pp. 205-33 in Cohen and Wartofsky [1965].

Radnitzky, G. (1976) 'Popperian Philosophy of Science as an Antidote Against Relativism', pp. 506-46 in Cohen, Feyerabend, and Wartofsky [1976].

Radnitzky, and Andersson, G. (1978) *Progress and Rationality in Science*, Dordrecht, Holland: Reidel.

Ravetz, J. (1971) *Scientific Knowledge and its Social Problems*, Oxford: Clarendon.

Remenyi, J.V. (1979) 'Core Demi-Core Interaction: Towards a General Theory of Disciplinary and Subdisciplinary Growth', *History of Political Economy*, 11, pp. 30-63.

Rizzo, M.J. (1982) 'Mises and Lakatos: A Reformulation of Austrian Methodology', pp. 53-73 in Kirzner [1982].

Rosenberg, A. (1979) 'Can Economic Theory Explain Everything?', *Philosophy of Social Sciences*, 9, pp. 509-29.

——— (1980) ' A Skeptical History of Microeconomic Theory', *Theory and Decision*, 12, pp. 79-93.

——— (1983) 'If Economics Isn't Science, What Is It?' *Philosophical Forum*, 14, pp. 296-314.

——— (1986) 'Lakatosian Consolations for Economics', *Economics and Philosophy*, 2, pp. 127-39.

Routh, G. (1987) *The Origin of Economic Ideas*, 2nd edn., London: Macmillan.

Salmon, W.C. (1975) *The Foundations of Scientific Inference*, Pittsburgh: Pittsburgh University Press

Sassower, R. (1986) *Philosophy of Economics : A Critique of Demarcation*, University Press of America.

Scheffler, I. (1967) *Science and Subjectivity*, Indianapolis, Ind. : Bobbs Merrill.

Schilpp, P.A. (ed.) (1974) *The Philosophy of Karl Popper*, LaSalle, Ill.: Open Court.

Schmidt, R.H. (1982) 'Methodology and Finance', *Theory and Decision*, 14, pp. 391-413.

Sen, A.K. (1967) 'The Nature and Classes of Prescriptive Judgements', *Philosophical Quarterly*, 17, pp. 46-62.

——— (1970) *Collective Choice and Social Welfare*, Amsterdam: North Holland.

Shapere, D. (1964) 'The Structure of Scientific Revolutions', *Philo-*

sophical Review, 73, pp. 383-94.
——— (1966) 'Meaning and Scientific Change', pp. 41-85 in Colodny (1966).
Shaw, W.H. (1978) *Marx's Theory of History*, London: Hutchinson.
Stewart, I.M.T. (1979) *Reasoning and Method in Economics: An Introduction to Economic Methodology*, London : McGraw-Hill.
Sugden, R. (1981) *The Political Economy of Public Choice*, Oxford: Martin Robertson.
Suppe, F. (ed.) (1977) *The Structure of Scientific Theories*, 2nd edn., Urbana: University of Illinois Press.
Suppes, P. *et al.* (eds) (1973) *Logic, Methodology and Philosophy of Science IV*, Amsterdam: North-Holland.
——— (1979) 'The Role of Formal Methods in the Philosophy of Science', pp. 16-27 in Asquith and Kyburg [1979].

Toulmin, S. (1970) 'Does the Distinction between Normal and Revolutionary Science Hold Water?', pp. 39-50 in Lakatos and Musgrave [1970].
——— (1972) *Human Understanding*, Vol. I, Princeton, N.J.: Princeton University Press.

Urbach, P. (1978) 'The Objective Promise of a Research Programme', pp. 99-113 in Radnitzky and Andersson [1978].

Watkins, J.W.N. (1958) 'Confirmable and Influential Metaphysics', *Mind*, 67, pp. 344-65.
——— (1970) 'Against "Normal Science"', pp. 25-37 in Lakatos and Musgrave [1970].
——— (1975) 'Metaphysics and the Advancement of Science', *British Journal for the Philosophy of Science*, 26, pp. 91-121.
——— (1978) 'The Popperian Approach to Scientific Knowledge', pp. 23-43 in Radnitzky and Andersson [1978].
——— (1984) *Science and Scepticism*, London : Hutchinson.
Weintraub, E.R. (1979) *Microfoundations*, Cambridge: Cambridge University Press.
——— (1985) 'Appraising General Equilibrium Analysis', *Economics and Philosophy*, 1, pp. 23-37.
Wisdom, J.O. (1963) 'The Refutability of "Irrefutable Laws"', *British Journal for the Philosophy of Science*, 13, pp. 303-6.
——— (1987a) *Challengeability in Modern Science*, Aldershot: Avebury.
——— (1987b) *Philosophy of the Social Sciences I: A Metascientific Introduction*, Aldershot: Avebury.

Wong, S. (1973) 'The "F-twist" and the Methodology of Paul Samuelson', *American Economic Review*, 62, pp. 312-25.

Worrall, J. (1978a) 'The Ways in Which the Methodology of Scientific Research Programmes Improves on Popper's Methodology', pp. 45-70 in Radnitzky and Andersson [1978].

——— (1978b) 'Research Programmes, Empirical Support, and the Duhem Problem: Replies to Criticism', pp. 321-38 in Radnitzky and Andersson [1978].

——— and Currie, G. (eds) (1978) *Imre Lakatos, Philosophical Papers*, 2 volumes, Cambridge: Cambridge University Press.

Zaher, E. (1978)' "Crucial" Experiments: A Case Study', pp. 71-97 in Radnitzky and Andersson [1978].

Index of Names

Index of Subjects